SUFISM

AN ACCOUNT OF THE
MYSTICS OF ISLAM

A. J. Arberry

DOVER PUBLICATIONS, INC.
Mineola, New York

Bibliographical Note

This Dover edition, first published in 2002, is an unabridged republication of a standard edition of the work originally published in 1950 by George Allen & Unwin Ltd., London.

Library of Congress Cataloging-in-Publication Data

Arberry, A. J. (Arthur John), 1905–1969.
    Sufism : an account of the mystics of Islam / A.J. Arberry.
       p. cm.
    Originally published: London : Allen & Unwin, [1950], in series: Ethical and religious classics of East and West ; no. 2.
    Includes bibliographical references and index.
    ISBN 0-486-41958-4 (pbk.)
     1. Sufism. I. Title.

BP189 .A7 2001
297.4–dc21

2001028671

Manufactured in the United States of America
Dover Publications, Inc., 31 East 2nd Street, Mineola, N.Y. 11501

GENERAL INTRODUCTION

As a result of two Wars that have devastated the world men and women everywhere feel a twofold need. We need a deeper understanding and appreciation of other peoples and their civilizations, especially their moral and spiritual achievements. And we need a new vision of the Universe, a clearer insight into the fundamentals of ethics and religion. How ought men to behave? How ought nations? Does God exist? What is His Nature? How is He related to His creation? Especially, how can man approach Him? In other words, there is a general desire to know what the greatest minds, whether of East or West, have thought and said about the Truth of God and of the beings who (as most of them hold) have sprung from Him, live by Him, and return to Him.

It is the object of this Series, which originated among a group of Oxford men and their friends, to place the chief ethical and religious masterpieces of the world, both Christian and non-Christian, within easy reach of the intelligent reader who is not an expert—the undergraduate, the ex-Service man who is interested in the East, the Adult Student, the intelligent public generally. The Series will contain books of three kinds: translations, reproductions of ethical and religious art, and Background Books showing the surroundings in which the literature and art arose and developed. These books overlap each other. Religious art, both in East and West, often illustrates a religious text, and in suitable cases the text and pictures will be printed together to complete each other. The Background Books will often consist largely of translations. The volumes will be prepared by scholars of distinction,

5

who will try to make them, not only scholarly, but intelligible and enjoyable.

Their contents will also be very varied—ethical and social, biographical, devotional, philosophic and mystical, whether in poetry, in pictures or in prose. There is a great wealth of material. Confucius lived in a time much like our own, when State was at war with State and the people suffering and disillusioned; and the "Classics" he preserved or inspired show the social virtues that may unite families, classes and States into one great family, in obedience to the Will of Heaven. Asoka and Akbar (both of them great patrons of art) ruled a vast Empire on the principles of religious faith. There are the moral anecdotes and moral maxims of the Jewish and Muslim writers of the Middle Ages. There are the beautiful tales of courage, love and fidelity in the Indian and Persian epics. Shakespeare's plays show that he thought the true relation between man and man is love. Here and there a volume will illustrate the unethical or less ethical man and the difficulties that beset him.

Then there are the devotional and philosophic works. The lives and legends (legends often express religious truth with clarity and beauty) of the Buddha, of the parents of Mary, of Francis of Assisi, and the exquisite sculptures and paintings that illustrate them. Indian and Christian religious music, and the words of prayer and praise which the music intensifies. There are the Prophets and Apocalyptic writers, Zarathustrian and Hebrew; the Greek philosophers and the Christian thinkers—Greek, Latin, Medieval and Modern—whom they so deeply influenced. There is too the Hindu, Buddhist and Christian teaching expressed in such great monuments as the Indian temples, Barabudur (the Chartres of Asia), and Ajanta, Chartres itself and the Sistine Chapel.

Finally there are the mystics of feeling, and the mystical

philosophers. In God-loving India the poets, musicians, sculptors and painters inspired by the spiritual worship of Krishna and Rama, as well as the philosophic mystics from the Upanishads onward. The two great Taoists, Lao-tze and Chuang-tze and the Sung mystical painters in China, Rūmī and other Sūfīs in Islam, Plato and Plotinus, followed by "Dionysius," Dante, Eckhart, Teresa and other great mystics and mystical painters in many Christian lands.

Mankind is hungry, but the feast is there, though it is locked up and hidden away. It is the aim of this Series to put it within reach, so that, like the heroes of Homer, we may stretch out our hands to the good cheer laid before us.

No doubt the great religions differ in fundamental respects. But they are not nearly so far from one another as they seem. We think they are further off than they are largely because we so often misunderstand and misrepresent them. Those whose own religion is dogmatic have often been as ready to learn from other teachings as those who are liberals in religion. Above all there is an enormous amount of common ground in the great religions, concerning too the most fundamental matters. There is frequent agreement on the Divine Nature; God is the One, Self-Subsisting Reality, knowing Himself, and therefore loving and rejoicing in Himself. Nature and finite spirits are in some way subordinate kinds of Being, or merely appearances of the Divine, the One. The Way of man's approach or return to God is in essence the same, in Christian and in non-Christian teaching. It has three stages: an ethical stage, then one of knowledge and love, leading to the mystical Union of the soul with God. Each stage will be illustrated in these volumes.

Something of all this may (it is hoped) be learnt from these books and pictures in this Series. Read and pondered with a desire to learn, they will help men and women to find "fullness of life," and peoples to live together in greater understanding and harmony. To-day the earth is beautiful, but men are disillusioned and afraid. But there will come a day, perhaps not a distant day, when there will be a Renaissance of man's spirit: when men will be innocent and happy amid the beauty of the world. For their eyes will be opened to see that egoism and strife are folly, that the Universe is Spiritual, and that men are the sons of God.

> They shall not hurt nor destroy
> In all my holy mountain:
> For all the earth shall be full of the knowledge of
>   the Lord
> As the waters cover the sea.

CONTENTS

ONE

INTRODUCTORY

It has become a platitude to observe that mysticism is essentially one and the same, whatever may be the religion professed by the individual mystic: a constant and unvarying phenomenon of the universal yearning of the human spirit for personal communion with God. Much labour and erudition however have also been expended upon the attempt to shew how one form of mysticism has been influenced by another; while proof is often difficult or even impossible in such elusive matters, it is generally agreed that no religious movement can come into being or develop without having contact with other established faiths or denominations which are bound to leave their impress upon the new creation of thought and emotion.

In giving a necessarily brief account of Sufism, which is the name given to the mysticism of Islam, it is proposed for the sake of brevity to accept these two propositions as proven; no time will therefore be wasted upon reviewing or restating the argument, in progress for more than a century, that the Sufis owed much or little of what they did or said to Christian, Jewish, Gnostic, Neoplatonic, Hermetic, Zoroastrian or Buddhist example. Having noted that the area in which Islam and Sufism originated and flourished is that which witnessed the rise and triumph or rout of several other creeds each with its own particular mysticism, we shall leave this fact to speak for itself, and confine our attention to presenting Sufism as if it were an isolated manifestation; viewing the movement from within as an aspect of Islam, as though these other factors which certainly determined its growth did not exist. By following this procedure it is hoped to draw a picture recognisable as a unity in itself, a picture of a mysticism developing out of a single creed and ritual, which may then be compared and contrasted with the mysticisms of other faiths and so be seen for what it really is. For while mysticism is undoubtedly a universal constant, its variations can be observed to be very clearly and characteristically shaped by the several religious systems upon which they were based. In this varied company Sufism may be defined as the mystical movement of an uncompromising Monotheism.

The central core of Islamic teaching is the doctrine that God is One, that He has no partners or equals to share or contest His Omnipotence, that He admits the right of none to vary His Decrees or intercede with His Judgments. Islam recognises no incarnate God, no Saviour; the matter lies between Allah the One Lord (*rabb*), and every man His creature and servant (*'abd*). A few men have been called to be God's Prophets, whose duty, from Adam to Muhammad, was simply to call mankind to Him. They are the vehicles of the Divine Message to humanity, which varies not from age to age or people to people. Otherwise the Prophets are men like other men, except as God has and may have willed them to be the recipients of His especial Grace and Favour. The Prophet is certainly not to be worshipped, for this would be polytheism (*shirk*) and infidelity (*kufr*), though he is obviously to be revered and imitated, since he has been spoken to by God and chosen by God to be His messenger.

For the Muslim, God's Message is wholly contained in the Koran, a volume of revelations sent down from time to time to the man 'Muhammad. This Book does not annul but rather confirms the Divine Message as preserved, though in a corrupt and distorted tradition, in the Holy Scriptures of the Jews and the Christians. The Koran is accordingly the supreme authority to which the Muslim mystic looks for guidance and justification.

The manner in which the Koran was revealed to Muhammad is naturally of great interest to the Sufi, for is it not a visible proof that God speaks to man? And since it is his ardent desire himself to hear the Voice of God, he must be concerned to know how it came about that the Founder of his faith was so privileged as to be throughout his prophethood in constant touch with his Creator. Therefore the Sufi is bound to study the life of Muhammad (*sīra*), to comprehend his code of conduct (*sunna*), and to be intimate with the Traditions (*hadīth*), handed down from generation to generation, first by word of mouth and later in writing, which are the unique and abundant source upon which he may draw for enlightenment. The *hadīth* is the second pillar after the Koran upon which he, like all Muslims, rests the fabric of his faith and life.

From the earliest days of Islam the Prophet lacked not for faithful followers who sought to copy his example and live righteously and humbly in the sight of God and man. The uprightness of their conduct and the fullness of their piety were so pleasing to their Creator that of His Infinite Goodness He chose them to be His "friends" (*auliyā'*, sing. *walī*), a term which afterwards became more or less synonymous with the Christian "saint". The Sufi, who desires earnestly to be admitted to like intimacy and privilege, is diligent in learning how these holy men conducted themselves publicly and in private, committing to mind and heart the words of wisdom and sanctity, the songs of devotion and heavenly love which were remembered of them. These he took for his third pillar.

Finally, in a life of sincere obedience to the Will of God, lived abstemiously and meditatively, guided by the Word of God, the Life of His Prophet, and the example of His saints, the Sufi is himself the recipient of such marks of favour as God may choose to vouchsafe him. Passing through the various states (*ahwāl*, sing. *hāl*) and stages (*maqāmāt*, sing. *maqām*) of the spiritual pilgrimage, he encounters many proofs of the special relationship in which he stands to God (*karāmāt*, "graces"). These personal experiences constitute the fourth pillar of his temple of righteousness.

So guided and favoured, the Muslim mystic may hope even in this mortal life to win a glimpse of immortality, by passing away from self (*fanā'*) into the consciousness of survival in God (*baqā'*). After death and judgment, he aspires to dwell forever with the angels and prophets, the saints and saved, in the near and blissful Presence of the Almighty.

TWO

THE WORD OF GOD

MUHAMMAD, the son of 'Abd Allah and Āmina of the aristocratic tribe of Quraish, was born at Mecca, in the year A.D. 571 according to Arab historians. His parents were noble but impoverished members of a proud clan; his father died before the infant was born, his mother when he was about six years old. He grew up in the protection first of his grandfather 'Abd al-Muttalib and then, when he died, of his uncle Abū Tālib, a trader. As a boy, Muhammad roamed the hills about Mecca watching over the family's flocks; thus early he grew accustomed to the loneliness of orphandom and the desolation of Arabia's arid wastes. At twenty-five he married Khadīja, a wealthy widow fifteen years his senior, and during her lifetime took no other partner; he was now for the first time comfortable in circumstance; he attended to his wife's business with scrupulous care and honesty.

Still in the intervals of his work he often retired to the hills which he had known so well as a poor lad. There, it is said, he meditated upon the cruel tribal strife which drenched the sands of Arabia in blood, the abominations of idolatry and licentiousness that reigned in the noisy towns. Towards his fortieth year he experienced a strange visitation which proved to be the beginning of his prophetic mission. Absorbed in thought within the cave of Hira, he suddenly heard a voice bidding him "Recite in the Name of thy Lord"[1]: a brief message followed which encouraged him to believe—for he was more or less familiar with Jewish tradition—that he had been called to prophesy to man. After an interval during which no further revelations

15

came (so that he began to be torn with doubts and mis-
givings), he presently received a yet clearer message.
Hurrying home in a state of extreme agitation, he begged
Khadīja to wrap him in a mantle; as he lay quiet and
attentive he heard the voice as urgent as before. "O thou
enwrapped in thy mantle, arise and warn!" [2] Thereafter,
and during the remainder of his earthly life which closed
in A.D. 632, Muhammad heard the voice—identified as
that of the angel Gabriel—at regular intervals. Whatever
he heard he repeated to his kinsmen and followers: in
course of time the series of revelations was gathered
together into a book and called the Koran—a word which
means "recitation" and is derived from the same root
as the first word he ever heard descending out of
heaven.

The Koran is a volume of scriptures consisting of many
varied elements ranging from apocalyptic admonition—
visions of heaven and hell and the summons to repent
betimes—to rhapsodic accounts of the missions of former
prophets, to ritual and legal ordinance. It is a confirma-
tion and not an abrogation of the revelations accorded by
God to earlier messengers, including Abraham who built
the Holy Shrine (Ka'ba) of Mecca, Moses the lawgiver of
the Jews, and Jesus son of Mary, Word of God, who was
not as the Christians alleged killed upon the Cross, a
simulacrum being divinely substituted for him.

While the Muslim Scriptures prescribe in detail the
religious duties incumbent upon the believer, and regulate
his behaviour as a servant of God and a member of the
faithful community, we are not immediately concerned
here to summarise these aspects of the Koran. We are
interested rather to examine those passages beloved by the
Sufis as testifying to God's Nature and Attributes, His
Self-revelation to mankind through the voice of Gabriel
speaking to Muhammad. For these mystical texts are the

chief encouragement and justification of the Sufi in his belief that he also may commune with God.

While God is presented throughout the Koran as the One Omnipotent Lord, "Master of the Day of Judgment,"[3] Omniscient beyond the understanding of men so that "they comprehend not aught of His knowledge,"[4] yet He repeatedly commands His servants to consider His works and contemplate His creation, for by that means He may be known as God. "Do they not look upon the camel, how she is created?"[5] God asks; and again, "Have they never looked up at the birds subjected to Him in Heaven's vault? None holdeth them in hand but God: in these are signs for such as believe."[6] The bee too furnishes "a sign for those who consider."[7] In a noble passage God proclaims, "Assuredly in the creation of the Heavens and of the Earth; and in the alternation of night and day; and in the ships which pass through the seas with things useful to man; and in the rain which God sendeth down from Heaven, giving life thereby to the earth after it was dead, scattering over it all manner of cattle; and in the change of the winds, and in the clouds that are made to do service between the Heaven and the Earth; in all these things are signs for those who understand."[8] So from the greatest and most majestic aspects of creation, to the least and lowliest: "Verily God is not ashamed to set forth as well the instance of a gnat."[9]

"If My servants enquire of thee concerning Me," God charges Muhammad, "lo, I am near"[10]; indeed, He is "nearer to him than his own jugular vein."[11] If a man would see the marvellous works of God, he is bidden to "journey through the earth, and see how He hath brought forth created beings"[12]—a command which the wandering friars of Islam took to heart, and quoted in support of their way of life. "Whithersoever ye turn, there is the Face of God"[13]: this most beloved of all texts has been the inspiration of many fine sayings and poems. But perhaps the most justly celebrated of all such passages is the so-called Light-Verse and those following it, the subject of constant meditation and commentary.

> God is the Light of the Heavens and of the Earth. His Light is like a niche wherein is a lamp, the lamp encased in glass, the glass as it were a glistening star. From a blessed tree it is lighted, the olive neither of the East nor of the West, whose oil would well nigh shine out, even though fire touched it not. It is light upon light. God guideth whom He will to His light, and God setteth forth parables to men, for God knoweth all things. In the temples which God hath allowed to be reared, that His Name may therein be remembered, do men praise Him morn and even: men whom neither merchandise nor traffic beguiles from the remembrance of God, and from the observance of prayer, and the payment of the stated alms, through fear of the day when hearts shall throb and eyes shall roll, that for their most excellent works God may recompense them, and of His bounty increase it to them more and more, for God maketh provision for whom He pleaseth without measure. But as to the infidels, their works are like the vapour in a plain which the thirsty dreameth to be water, until when he cometh unto it, he findeth it not aught, but findeth that God is with him; and He fully payeth him his account: for swift to account is God: or like the darkness on the deep sea when covered by billows riding upon billows, above which are clouds: darkness upon darkness. When a man reacheth forth his hand, he well nigh cannot see it! He to whom God shall not give light, no light at all hath he. Hast thou not seen how all in the Heavens and in the Earth uttereth the praise of God?—the very birds as they spread their wings? Every creature knoweth its prayer and its praise: and God knoweth what they do.   God's is the kingdom of the Heavens and of the Earth: and unto God shall be the final return. [14]

God spoke of old to every prophet in turn, each according to his especial mark of favour: "to Moses and

Aaron the illumination, and a light and a warning for the God-fearing";[15] "unto Abraham his direction, for We knew him worthy";[16] "and We gave Solomon insight into the affair, and on both of them (David and Solomon) We bestowed wisdom and insight; and We constrained the mountains and the birds to join with David in Our praise, and to Solomon We subjected the strongly blowing wind: it sped at his bidding to the land We had blessed."[17] God spoke to Moses through the miracle of the burning bush;[18] "and when Moses came at Our set time and his Lord spake with him, he said, 'O Lord, shew Thyself to me, that I may look upon Thee.' He said, 'Thou shalt not see Me; but look towards the mountain, and if it abide firm in its place, then shalt thou see Me.' And when God manifested Himself to the mountain He turned it into dust; and Moses fell in a swoon."[19]

So in due time Muhammad too was vouchsafed a wonderful mark of Divine favour, when "He carried His servant by night from the sacred temple (of Mecca) to the temple that is more remote (of Jerusalem) whose precincts We have blessed, that We might shew him of Our signs."[20] Concerning this miraculous journey a wealth of pious legend grew up to which reference will be made later; for the present it suffices to refer to another passage in the Koran which is commonly taken as expanding upon the very brief hint just quoted, and describing visions of Gabriel experienced by Muhammad on two separate occasions. "It is naught but a revelation that was revealed: one terrible in power taught it him, endued with wisdom. Evenly poised he stood in the highest part of the horizon: then came he nearer and approached, and was at the distance of two bow-shots, or even closer. And He revealed to His servant what He revealed; his heart falsified not what he saw. Do ye then dispute with him concerning what he saw? He had seen him also another time, near the Sidra-tree which marks the boundary, near which is the garden of repose. When the Sidra-tree was covered with what covered it, his eye turned not aside, nor did it wander, for he saw the greatest of the signs of his Lord." [21] Some commentators took these mysterious words to signify an actual vision of God; but this question came to be fraught with grave theological problems, and the more cautious view inclined to the theory that the reference was to angels, or a sheet of gold. It has remained a subject of serious dispute whether Muhammad was in the flesh or the spirit when he saw these wonders.

If it should be objected that the foregoing marvels were accorded to prophets only, who are by definition specially privileged among men—and Muhammad being the Seal of the Prophets, none after him may hope to be favoured by God in like manner—yet the Koran has a message no less encouraging for every individual man. For man, by virtue of his descent from Adam, is created higher than the angels; for him indeed was all creation made. "He it is Who created for you all that is on Earth, then proceeded to the Heaven, and into seven Heavens did He fashion it: and He knoweth all things. When thy Lord said to the angels, 'Verily, I am about to place one in my stead (*khalīfa*) on earth', they said, 'Wilt thou place there one who will do ill therein and shed blood, when we celebrate Thy praise and extol Thy holiness?' God said, 'Verily, I know what ye know not.' And He taught Adam the names of all things, and then set them before the angels, and said, 'Tell Me the names of these, if ye are endued with wisdom.' They said, 'Praise be to Thee! We have no knowledge but what Thou hast given us to know. Thou, Thou art the Knowing, the Wise.' He said, 'O Adam, inform them of their names.' And when he had informed them of their names, He said, 'Did I not say to you that I know the hidden things of the Heavens and of the Earth, and that I know what ye bring to light, and what ye hide?' And when We said to the angels, 'Bow down and worship Adam,' then worshipped they all, save Eblis. He refused and swelled with pride, and became one of the unbelievers."[22]

Not only was man created in order that he might be God's viceregent in the earth; even before he or aught else was made, man entered into an eternal covenant (mīthāq) to worship God as the One Lord. "And when thy Lord brought forth their descendants from the reins of the sons of Adam, and took them to witness against themselves, 'Am I not', said He, 'your Lord?' They said, 'Yea, we witness it'."[23] We shall see how in later times this verse, interpreted as referring to an event which took place in pre-eternity, served as the focal point in an elaborate theosophy.

"Adore, and draw thou nigh"[24]: these were the last words uttered by the Voice in the first revelation of all. Elsewhere in the Koran we are told that every godly act of man is preceded by an act of God's favour towards man. "Then He turned to them, that they might turn",[25] He said, referring to three backsliders among Muhammad's immediate followers who repented. "God was well pleased with them, and they were well pleased with God"[26]: so God describes the blessed saints in Paradise; for "He loveth them, and they love Him".[27] This last text is of great significance as supporting the Sufi doctrine of love (mahabba) and as providing the ultimate authority for the idea of a trinity of Lover, Loved and Love. The conception of a remote, indifferent Potentate of the Universe is wholly overthrown by this picture of the Merciful Allah ever taking the first step towards man, the elect of His creation, to draw him unto Him by the powerful cords of love.

Yet more; there is a passage, relating to the victorious battle of Badr, where God says, "So it was not ye who slew them, but God slew them; thou didst not cast when thou didst cast, but God cast". [28] These words, constantly meditated, seemed to the Sufi conclusive evidence that God even acts through the instrumentality of man when He finds man worthy to become His instrument. Just as the miracle of the gravelstones and dust scattered by God into the eyes of the Meccans at Badr decisively influenced the issue in the struggle between faith and unbelief, so at all times God is able and ready to work wonders, in the persons of His saints, to prove the realities of true religion.

The foregoing are some of the passages in the Koran into which the Sufis read a mystical significance; there are many others besides, too numerous for quotation and too elusive in the ordinary way to carry much conviction, which are sprinkled through the pages of the Sufi books as testimony to their teachings. "Remember God often" is a phrase which constantly recurs in the Koran: in its context it has an obvious, neutral meaning, but the Sufis interpreted it in a special way, and the word "remembrance" (*dhikr*) acquired in time a very particular connotation. "Every thing upon the earth passeth away, save His face" [29] seems where it stands to be innocent of all but its apparent intention; it is taken by the Sufis as the peg upon which to hang their characteristic doctrine of the passing away (*fanā'*) of human attributes through Union with God, whereby the mystic achieves the eternal continuance (*baqā'*) of spiritual life in Him.

To understand the extreme lengths to which the Sufis were prepared to go in reading esoteric meanings into the quite simple language of their Scriptures, it is necessary to remember that the Koran was committed to memory by all deeply religious men and women, and recited constantly, aloud or in the heart; so that the mystic was in a state of uninterrupted meditation upon the Holy Book. Many passages which would otherwise pass without special notice were therefore bound to arrest their attention, already sufficiently alert, and to quicken their imagination, already fired by the discipline of their austerities and the rigour of their internal life. Minds naturally subtle—for the Arabs and Persians proved apt disciples of Aristotle and Plotinus—found no difficulty in applying to the Koran those methods whereby Philo had philosophised the Pentateuch. Finally the very style of the Muslim Scriptures—rhapsodic, nervous, highly rhetorical —proved ideally suited to such extravagances of interpretation; while its occasional real obscurities, which provided orthodox exegetes with so much opportunity to display their lexicographical learning, added further fuel to the flame of mystic fervour. The esoteric exposition of the Koran became a central point in the hard training of the Sufi.

THREE

THE LIFE OF THE PROPHET

CONTEMPORARY information on the life of the founder of Islam is confined—apart from such hints as the Koran itself offers—to anecdotes or "traditions" (*hadīth*) ascribed to one or other of his many early followers and handed down from generation to generation in a chain of transmission. It was not until the second century of the new faith that serious attempts began to be made to collect and codify this extremely varied and scattered material. The *hadīth* acquired ever greater importance as the theology and religious law of Islam, already from earliest times the subject of ardent debate and bitter dispute, made increasing demands upon such sources of evidence as might supplement the insufficiently detailed authority of the Koran. The religion now being torn by faction and schism, it became the interest of partisan champions of the clashing viewpoints to gather up—or, as their opponents were quick to allege, invent—Prophetic sanctions to support their rival claims.

The third century (or the ninth by Christian reckoning) produced the great canonical collections of *hadīth*, notably those of al-Bukhārī (d.256/870) and Muslim (d.261/875). These were accepted by the accredited theologians and lawyers as comprising all the traditions whose authenticity had stood the searching test of historical scholarship applied with a rigorous zeal for orthodoxy. By this time the Sufi movement was firmly established, and the mystics had assembled many traditions favourable to their own outlook which failed to qualify for admission to the canon. This is not to say, of course, that the Sufis did not also draw to a very considerable extent upon the accepted corpus of *hadīth* as well; but it is always the eccentric that attracts most attention, and when in due course Sufism encountered the hostility of those who suspected the soundness of its doctrines and practices, the Sufis were liable to be condemned as weak in Tradition.

When we examine the sayings and anecdotes connected by the Sufis with Muhammad, we find that a substantial proportion of the most telling—from their point of view—is rejected by Bukhārī and Muslim. This need not wholly disconcert us, however, when we remember that Bukhārī "selected out of the 600,000 traditions he collected from 1000 sheikhs in the course of sixteen years of travel and labour in Persia, al-'Iraq, Syria, al-Hijaz and Egypt some 7275."[1] All the same it is important to have in mind that by the highest standards of Muslim scholarship this material, of fundamental significance to the Sufi, is suspect. As in the preceding chapter, we shall here cite some characteristic examples of the *hadīth* which are most frequently upon the lips of Sufi writers and apologists as justifying various aspects of their teachings, not entering into the controversy whether the examples quoted are the genuine utterance of Muhammad or not. We shall divide the material into two parts, representing the ascetic and the theosophical tendencies of Sufism, remarking that the "ascetic" traditions are, as might be expected, far less suspect in the eyes of orthodoxy than the "theosophical."

"Poverty is my pride." This saying of Muhammad, afterwards taken as the watchword of many Sufi orders, reflects the generally accepted view that the founder of Islam lived lowly and humbly all his days, and that the great power and increasing riches which accrued to him in the later years of his mission did not change the austerity of his habits. The Prophet is said to have prayed, "O God, make me live lowly and die lowly and rise from the dead among the lowly"; he also said, "On the Day of Resurrection God will say, 'Bring ye My loved ones nigh unto Me'; then the angels will say, 'Who are Thy loved ones?' and God will answer them, saying, 'The poor and destitute.'" [2] There is abundant authority in the Koran for the view that the amassing of worldly possessions is displeasing to God: "The life of this world is but a sport, and a play, and a gaud, something to boast about among yourselves." [3] To Muhammad the Final Judgment seemed a near reality, and he constantly urged his followers to abstain from material pleasures in order to lay up treasure in Heaven. "Do not strain thine eye after the good things wherewith We have provided a few of them—the gauds of the present life, to try them thereby" [4]: riches were given by God to a few men, not as a mark of superior worth or favour, but to prove their faith. An angel is said to have come down to the Prophet out of heaven with a message from God, saying, "These are the keys of the treasures of the earth, that they may be thine, both gold and silver: in them thou mayst dwell until the Day of Resurrection, and they shall in no wise lessen the portion that is laid up for thee with God." But the Prophet rejected the proffered riches, saying, "Once I hunger, and once I am filled," counting this offer to be a testing and a trial from God. [5]

Poverty brings out two virtues: it encourages abstemiousness and the eschewing of unlawful pleasure, and it stimulates trust in God. The Prophet once said to Hāritha, an illustrious Companion, "How farest thou this day, O Hāritha?" He replied, "Believing truly, O Messenger of God." "And what," asked the Prophet, "is the truth of thy belief?" Hāritha answered, "I have turned my soul away from this world. Therefore I have thirsted by day, and watched by night, and it is as though I behold the Throne of my Lord coming forth, and the people of

Paradise taking joy together, and the people of Hell making moan together." The Prophet said, "A believer whose heart God has illumined: thou hast known, so hold fast."[6]

Faith is of little value, unless the believer has such trust in God that he confides in Him wholly, and leaves all his affairs in God's hands. The Prophet said, "If ye trusted in God as ye should, He would sustain you even as He sustains the birds, which in the morning go forth hungry, and return in the evening filled."[7] It is sincere trust (*tawakkul*) that converts the fear natural to the heart of sinful man into an abundant hope of God's forgiveness; it sustains him in adversity, and humbles him when prosperous, so that he continues all his days well pleased with God, a state which we have seen from the Koran to be symptomatic of God's pleasure with His servant.[8] The Prophet relates in one of his descriptions of Paradise how the blessed there petition for God's good pleasure, and God replies, "It is My good pleasure that hath made you to dwell within My house, and to attain My blessing."[9]

As trust, leading to satisfaction (*ridā*), brings man for the first time into a partnership of spiritual emotion with God, so it leads on to the yet higher sentiment of loving God, a state similarly preceded by a like disposition on God's part.[10] The Prophet said, "God said, In no way does My servant so draw nigh Me as when performing those duties which I have imposed on him; and My servant continues to draw near to Me through works of supererogation, until I love him. And when I love him, I am his ear, so he hears by Me, and his eye, so that he sees by Me, and his tongue, so that he speaks by Me, and his hand, so that he takes by Me."[11] This celebrated Tradition forms the basis of an elaborate structure of mystical theosophy in the writings of the later Sufis. Love is indeed

the gateway leading from the ascetic and contemplative
to the unitive life.

The love of God for man proves the uniqueness of man
in all the world of creation. The Prophet reported God as
saying, "My Earth and My Heaven contain Me not, but
the heart of My faithful servant containeth Me."[12] Again,
God is stated to have said, "I was a hidden treasure, and I
desired to be known; therefore I created the creation in
order that I might be known."[13] These famous words are
taken by the Sufis to refer especially to man, the object of
God's love—that is, of course, the Ideal Man—who is thus
the mirror in which God's Attributes may be seen.
Muhammad is even said to have declared, "He that hath
seen me hath seen God."[14] There being in every man
that which God loves, it behoves the mystic to examine
himself constantly until he truly knows himself, for
"Whoso knows himself, knows his Lord."[15] "Consult thy
heart," the Prophet said to one of his followers, "and thou
wilt hear the secret ordinance of God proclaimed by the
heart's inward knowledge, which is real faith and
divinity."[16] On another occasion he said, "Beware of the
discernment of the true believer, for he sees by the light
of God."[17] By loving God and knowing God, the faithful
can realise supernatural powers; for the Prophet said, "If
ye knew God as He ought to be known, ye would walk
on the seas, and the mountains would move at your
call."[18]

We have referred above to the Night Journey (isrā') of
Muhammad, which for the Sufis constitutes the Prophet's
supreme mystical experience and an example which they
may aspire to follow. It is therefore not without significance
that Abu 'l-Qāsim al-Qushairī (d.465/1074), author of
the most famous and authoritative treatise on Sufism in
Arabic, wrote a separate work on this theme in which he
collected together several versions of the Ascent (mi'rāj)

together with the comments of celebrated Sufis on the enigmatic references to the event which are contained in the Koran. The legend is recounted in considerable detail in all the canonical collections of *hadīth*, but without the esoteric embroidery with which the Sufis embellished it. We read that one evening Muhammad, while "in a state between sleeping and waking," was borne up on a winged horse called Burāq to the Seventh Heaven and the Near Presence of God, being accompanied on all but the last part of the journey by Gabriel. Upon the way he met the earlier prophets who without exception acknowledged his superiority, and the supremacy of his community over all others; finally he was privileged to hear the Voice of God proceeding from the Throne. When he said, "O God, I know not how to utter Thy praise," God answered, "O Muhammad, if thou speakest not, I will speak; if thou deemest thyself unworthy to praise Me, I will make the universe thy deputy, that all its atoms may praise Me in thy name."[19] Some went so far as to declare that upon this night Muhammad actually saw God, but this report was denied by 'Ā'isha the Prophet's favourite wife, and rejected by the majority of Sufis who held to the orthodox opinion that God has never been seen in this world.[20]

It was with reference to this miraculous experience that the Prophet said, "I am not as one of you; verily I pass the night with my Lord, and He gives me food and drink," and on another occasion he declared, "I am with God in a state in which none of the Cherubim nor any Prophet is capable of being contained with me."[21] In an ecstasy of bliss Muhammad prayed to God, "Do not transport me to yonder world of affliction! Do not throw me under the sway of nature and passion." But God replied, "It is My decree that thou shalt return to the world for the sake of establishing the religious law, in order that I may give thee there what I have given thee here." When he returned

to this world, he used to say as often as he felt a longing
for that exalted station, "O Bilāl, comfort us by the call
to prayer!" Thus to him every time of prayer was an
Ascension and a new nearness to God.[22]

FOUR

THE ASCETICS

Now I will tell a tale of long ago,
How first the Faith began, and how it grew
To full perfection; yea, and I will tell
How next it withered, till it hath become
E'en as a faded garment. After this
I have for thee a very gem of knowledge
Which thou canst gain, if thou wilt heed my words,
A knowledge copious, to scour the heart
Of stain and rust, and make it clean and bright.
True is my knowledge, clear and eloquent,
Precious as pearls and rubies of great price;
By Grace Divine I indicate the truth,
Being taught by God Himself, for that I live
Within an age become exceeding strange,
Cruel, and terrible, wherein we need
Most urgently a statement of our faith
And intellectual arguments thereto:
Islam hath been most nobly eulogized—
As mourners praise the dear, departed dead!

These lines were written by Ahmad b. 'Āsim al-Antākī of Antioch, who was born at Wasit (Iraq) in 140/757 and died at Damascus in 215/830; they represent very well the mood of religious men in the early days of the Abbasid caliphate. The far-flung conquests of the first century of Islam brought immense power and wealth to the hands of men not of the Prophet's House, who exercised sway over vast territories and in their palaces lived a life of ease and luxury that scandalised simpler souls.

Muhammad's immediate companions and followers are pictured in pious legend as innocent of these excesses; despite their position of privilege, they maintained the

simple dignity and austerity of habit which they had
learned from the Prophet.

> When Abū Bakr succeeded to the leadership, and the
> world in its entirety came to him in abasement, he did
> not lift up his head on that account, or make any pre-
> tensions; he wore a single garment, which he used to pin
> together, so that he was known as the 'man of the two
> pins.' 'Umar b. al-Khattab, who also ruled the world in
> its entirety, lived on bread and olive-oil; his clothes
> were patched in a dozen places, some of the patches
> being of leather; and yet there were opened unto him
> the treasures of Chosroes and Caesar. As for 'Uthman, he
> was like one of his slaves in dress and appearance; of him
> it is related that he was seen coming out of one of his
> gardens with a faggot of firewood on his shoulders, and
> when questioned on the matter he said, 'I wanted to see
> whether my soul would refuse.' When 'Ali succeeded to
> the rule, he bought a waistband for four dirhams and a
> shirt for five dirhams; finding the sleeve of his garment too
> long, he went to a cobbler and taking his knife cut off the
> sleeve level with the tips of his fingers; yet this same man
> divided the world right and left.[1]

So the "Righteous Caliphs" appeared to al-Kharrāz,
famous mystic of the third/ninth century; and the report of
their holiness was widely accepted. With the succession of
the cunning Mu'āwiya (661-80) all was changed; worldly
considerations supplanted spiritual aspiration as the
basis of government; while Mu'āwiya's son and heir Yazīd
(680-3) was a confirmed drunkard. The transference of
the capital from Mecca to Damascus was itself symptomatic of this decline in piety; the enervating effeminacy of
Syria replaced the ascetic manliness of Arabia. When in
due course an extravagant new capital, Baghdad, was
built on the ruins of the old Persian empire in a land where
Arabic was almost a second language, the course of
degeneracy was fully run.

In these circumstances nothing was left to the religiously

minded but more and more to withdraw from a society
which was obviously on the road to damnation. Many of
those who had seen the Prophet were compelled to take
this, the only way left open to them, in their later years to
register their horror at corruption in high places. Secure
in the conviction of their own righteousness, they did not
fear to thunder denunciation and threaten the imminence
of Divine punishment; and it became the well approved
diversion of puritanical circles to listen to the eloquent
jeremiads of the ancient faithful.

There was one honourable exception to the rule of
caliphal ungodliness in the person of 'Umar b. 'Abd al-
'Azīz (717-20), who is praised not only for his own virtuous
conduct but also because he corresponded with al-Hasan
al-Basrī (d.110/728), an eminent early theologian renowned for his piety and asceticism, who is claimed by the
Sufis as one of their first and most distinguished partisans.
The tenor of al-Hasan's message, which may be taken as
typical of the ascetics of the first age and has in it nothing
of the theosophy which developed later, is illustrated by
some passages from a letter which he wrote to his exalted
patron. [2]

Beware of this world with all wariness; for it is like to
a snake, smooth to the touch, but its venom is deadly. Turn
away from whatsoever delights thee in it, for the little
companioning thou wilt have of it; put off from thee its
cares, for that thou hast seen its sudden chances, and
knowest for sure that thou shalt be parted from it; endure
firmly its hardships, for the ease that shall presently be
thine. The more it pleases thee, the more do thou be wary
of it; for the man of this world, whenever he feels secure in
any pleasure thereof, the world drives him over into some
unpleasantness, and whenever he attains any part of it
and squats him down upon it, the world suddenly turns
him upside down. And again, beware of this world, for
its hopes are lies, its expectations false; its easefulness is

all harshness, muddied its limpidity. And therein thou art in peril: or bliss transient, or sudden calamity, or painful affliction, or doom decisive. Hard is the life of a man if he be prudent, dangerous if comfortable, being wary ever of catastrophe, certain of his ultimate fate. Even had the Almighty not pronounced upon the world at all, nor coined for it any similitude, nor charged men to abstain from it, yet would the world itself have awakened the slumberer, and roused the heedless; how much the more then, seeing that God has Himself sent us a warning against it, an exhortation regarding it! For this world has neither worth nor weight with God; so slight it is, it weighs not with God so much as a pebble or a single clod of earth; as I am told, God has created nothing more hateful to Him than this world, and from the day He created it He has not looked upon it, so much He hates it. It was offered to our Prophet with all its keys and treasures, and that would not have lessened him in God's sight by so much as the wing of a gnat, but he refused to accept it; and nothing prevented him from accepting it—for there is naught that can lessen him in God's sight—but that he knew that God hated a thing, and therefore he hated it, and God despised a thing, and he despised it, and God abased a thing, and he abased it. Had he accepted it, his acceptance would have been a proof that he loved it; but he disdained to love what his Creator hated, and to exalt what his Sovereign had debased. As for Muhammad, he bound a stone upon his belly when he was hungry; and as for Moses, the skin of his belly shewed as green as grass because of it all: he asked naught of God, the day he took refuge in the shade, save food to eat when he was hungered, and it is said of him in the stories that God revealed to him, 'Moses, when thou seest poverty approaching, say, Welcome to the badge of the righteous! and when thou seest wealth approaching, say, Lo! a sin whose punishment has been put on aforetime.' If thou shouldst wish, thou mightest name as a third the Lord of the Spirit and the Word (Jesus), for in his affair there is a marvel; he used to say, 'My daily bread is hunger, my badge is fear, my raiment is wool, my mount is my foot, my lantern at night is the moon, my fire by day is the sun, and my fruit and fragrant herbs are such things as the earth brings forth for the wild beasts and cattle. All the night I have nothing, yet there is none richer than I!' And if thou shouldst wish, thou mightest name as a fourth David, who was no less wonderful than these; he ate barley bread in his chamber, and fed his family upon bran meal, but his people on fine corn; and when it was night, he clad himself in sackcloth, and chained his hand to his neck, and wept until the dawn; eating coarse food, and wearing robes of hair. All these hated what God hates, and despised what God despises; then the righteous thereafter followed in their path and kept close upon their tracks.

Here we already see the establishment of an important Sufi theory, that poverty and abstinence were practised by the prophets themselves; and it is interesting to note how al-Hasan al-Basrī attributed to Jesus and David the austere practices which presently characterised so distinctively the Sufi ascetics, even to the wearing of wool. Ibn Sīrīn (d.110/728), a celebrated scholar contemporary with al-Hasan who attacked the latter's teachings and habits on many accounts,[3] in particular condemned the wearing of wool (sūf), which was already being affected by certain devotees, as being an imitation of Jesus, saying that "he preferred to follow the example of our Prophet who clothed himself in cotton."[4] The nickname Sufi, which is undoubtedly derived from the Arabic word for wool, appears to have been applied in the first place to a certain Abū Hāshim 'Uthmān b. Sharīk of Kufa, who died about the year 160/776; by the middle of the third/ninth century it had become the regular appellation of those who practised austerity; in the fourth/tenth century it also acquired a theosophical connotation.[5]

From Basra and Kufa the ascetic movement spread to all parts of the Islamic world, notably to Khorasan which during the second half of the second/eighth century became an important focus of political and religious

activity; it was in Khorasan that the plot was hatched
which overthrew the Umayyads and established the
Abbasid caliphate. To this remote province, which had
once been a flourishing centre of Buddhism, belonged
the celebrated Ibrāhīm b. Adham, prince of Balkh
(d.160/777), the legend of whose conversion to austerity
became a favourite theme among later Sufis and has often
been compared with the story of Gautama Buddha.

'My father was of Balkh,' Ibrāhīm b. Adham is reported
to have said, [6] 'and he was one of the kings of Khorasan. He
was a man of wealth, and taught me to love hunting. One
day I was out riding with my dog, when a hare or a fox
started. I pricked on my horse; then I heard a voice
behind me saying, 'It was not for this thou wast created:
it was not this thou wast charged to do.' I stopped, and
looked right and left, but saw no one; and I said, 'God
curse the devil!' Then I pricked on my horse again; and
I heard a voice clearer than before, 'O Ibrāhīm! It was
not for this thou wast created: it was not this thou wast
charged to do.' I stopped once more, and looked right
and left, and still I saw no one; and I repeated, 'God
curse the devil!' Then I pricked on my horse once more;
and I heard a voice from the bow of my saddle, 'O
Ibrāhīm! It was not for this thou wast created: it was not
this thou wast charged to do.' I stopped, and said, 'I have
been roused! I have been roused! A warning has come to
me from the Lord of the Worlds. Verily, I will not disobey
God from this day on, so long as the Lord shall preserve
me.' Then I returned to my people, and abandoned my
horse; I came to one of my father's shepherds, and took
his robe and cloak, and put my raiment upon him. Then
I went towards Iraq, wandering from land to land.

The story goes on to describe how he roamed from place
to place seeking a way of living "lawfully," until for a
time he earned his daily bread working as a gardener in
Syria; but presently his identity was discovered, and so
he went out to live in the desert. There he fell in with

Christian anchorites, from whom he learned the true knowledge of God.

'I learned gnosis (*ma'rifa*),' he related to a disciple,[7] "from a monk called Father Simeon. I visited him in his cell, and said to him, 'Father Simeon, how long hast thou been in thy cell here?' 'For seventy years,' he answered. 'What is thy food?' I asked. 'O Hanifite,' he countered, 'what has caused thee to ask this?' 'I wanted to know,' I replied. Then he said, 'Every night one chick-pea.' I said, 'What stirs thee in thy heart, so that this pea suffices thee?' He answered, 'They come to me one day in every year, and adorn my cell, and process about it, so doing me reverence; and whenever my spirit wearies of worship, I remind it of that hour, and endure the labours of a year for the sake of an hour. Do thou, O Hanifite, endure the labour of an hour, for the glory of eternity.' Gnosis then descended into my heart.

A disciple asked Ibrāhīm b. Adham for a definition of service, and he replied, "The beginning of service is meditation and silence, save for the recollection (*dhikr*) of God."[8] On another occasion, being informed that a certain man was studying grammar, he commented, "He is in greater need of studying silence."[9] He is said to have prayed, "O God, Thou knowest, that Paradise weighs not with me so much as the wing of a gnat. If Thou befriendest me by Thy recollection, and sustainest me with Thy love, and makest it easy for me to obey Thee, then give Thou Paradise to whomsoever Thou wilt."[10] In a letter to one of his fellow ascetics he wrote as follows.[11]

I charge thee to fear God, Who may not be disobeyed, and in Whom alone is thy hope. Fear God; for he that fears God is great and mighty, his hunger is satisfied and his thirst is quenched, and his mind is exalted above the world. His body is indeed seen to dwell among the peoples of this world, but his heart is face to face with the world to come. When the eye beholds the love of this

world, the sight of the heart is extinguished; wherefore a
man will loathe the unlawful things of this world and
eschew its lusts, yea, and he will abstain even from such
things as are lawful and pure, except for such shreds as
he needs to bind his loins and clothe his nakedness, and
then only the thickest and roughest he can find. He has
no trust nor hope save in God; his trust and hope are exalted
above every created thing, and repose in the Creator of
all things. He labours and exhausts himself, and wears
out his body for God's sake, so that his eyes are sunken
and his ribs stare; and God requites him therefor with
increase of intellect and strength of heart, and all the
things besides that He has stored up for him in the world
to come. Then spurn the world, my brother; for love of
the world makes a man deaf and blind, and enslaves him.
Say not 'to-morrow' or 'the day after to-morrow'; for
those that perished, perished because they abode always
in their hopes, until the truth came upon them suddenly in
their heedlessness, and wilful as they were they were
carried to their dark, narrow graves, abandoned by all
their kith and kin. Devote thyself to God with a penitent
heart, and an undoubting resolve. Farewell!

The Khorasanian school of asceticism was continued by
Ibrāhīm b. Adham's pupil Shaqīq of Balkh (d.194/810),
said by some authorities to have been the first to define
trust in God (*tawakkul*) as a mystical state (*hāl*).[12] The
story of his conversion as told by his grandson is interesting as shewing again the contacts between Islam and other
religions at this time, and the influence such contacts
were felt to have exercised upon the development of
Sufism.[13]

My grandfather owned three hundred villages on the
day he was killed at Washgird, yet he had not even a
winding-sheet to be buried in, for he had given everything
away. His raiment and sword are hung up to this hour,
and men touch them for a blessing. He had gone into the
lands of the Turks to do trade as a young man, among a
people called the Khusūsīya, who worshipped idols. He

went into their temple and there met their teacher, who
had shaved his head and beard and wore scarlet robes.
Shaqīq said to him, 'This upon which thou art engaged is
false; these men, and thou, and all creation—all have a
Creator and a Maker, there is naught like unto Him;
to Him belongs this world, and the next; He is Omnipotent, All-providing.' The servitor said to him, 'Thy words
do not accord with thy deeds.' Shaqiq said, 'How is that?'
The other replied, 'Thou hast asserted that thou hast a
Creator, Who is All-providing and Omnipotent; yet thou
hast exiled thyself to this place in search of thy provision.
If what thou sayest is true, He Who has provided for thee
here is the same as He Who provides for thee there; so
spare thyself this trouble.' Shaqīq said, 'The cause of my
abstinence (*zuhd*) was the remark of that Turk.' And he
returned, and gave away all he possessed to the poor, and
sought after knowledge.

In Shaqīq's discourse, so much of it as is preserved by
later writers, we discern the beginnings of a formal system
of self-discipline, such as the Sufis of the third/ninth
century developed much further. His pupil Hātim al-
Asamm (d.237/852), himself a noted member of the school
of Khorasan, quoted him to the following effect.[14]

If a man continued alive for two hundred years and
did not know these four things, he should not (God
willing) escape from Hell:—first, the knowledge (*maʿrifa*)
of God; second, the knowledge of himself; third, the knowledge of God's commandment and prohibition; fourth,
the knowledge of God's adversary and his own. The
interpretation of the knowledge of God is, that thou
knowest in thy heart that there is no other who gives and
withholds, hurts and advantages. Knowledge of self is
to know thyself, that thou canst not hurt or advantage,
and that thou hast not the power to do anything at all;
and likewise to oppose the self, which means, to be sub-
missive to God. Knowledge of God's commandment and
prohibition is to be aware that God's commandment rules
over thee and that thy provision depends upon God, and
to trust in this provision, being sincere in all thy actions;

and the sign of such sincerity is not to have in thee two characteristics, namely covetousness and impatience. Knowledge of God's adversary means being aware that thou hast an enemy, and that God will not accept from thee anything save it be as a result of warfare; and the warfare of the heart consists in making war against the enemy, and striving with him, and exhausting him.

Typical also of the Persian school of asceticism is 'Abd Allah b. al-Mubārak of Merv (d.181/797), claimed by the Sufis as one of them, who wrote a book on self-denial (*Kitāb al-Zuhd*) which has survived.[15] It consists of a collection of *hadīth* relating to abstinence, and is therefore of some importance not only as being the earliest of such specialised collections but also because it shews the ascetic at work assembling evidence in the Prophet's life and preaching to justify his own. A somewhat later native of Merv was Bishr b. al-Hārith al-Hāfī ("Barefoot") (d.227/841), who in his own words was "a rogue, a gangster" before he heard the call to God.[16] He taught a doctrine of indifference to the opinions of other men that foreshadows a later development in Sufism, the Malāma-tīya movement which came to acquire much notoriety. Bishr is reported to have said, "Conceal your virtuous actions, as you conceal your evil deeds,"[17] and again, "If thou art able to be in a situation where men will suppose thee to be a thief, by all means contrive to be so."[18] He wrote to a disciple as follows.[19]

Return to the course that is nearer to thee, namely to please thy Lord; let not thy heart revert to the applause or reproof of the people of thy time. Those thou fearest are indeed dead, except the righteous whose hearts are irradiated with life. For thou dwellest in a place where dead men are, amongst the graves of men living indeed, but dead to the world to come, whose footsteps are all obliterated from its paths. These are the people of thy time: wherefore hide thyself from that place where God's light never shines. Be not concerned if any man desert thee, and despair not over losing him, for it is more fortunate for thee to have them afar than to have them nigh thee; let God be thy sufficiency, take Him for thy associate, and let Him be the substitute for them. Beware of the people of thy time: it is not good to live with any that men to-day think well of, nor with any they think ill of either. It is better to die alone, than to live; for if any man thinks he can escape from evil and from the fear of temptation, let him know that there is no escape for him; if thou givest them power over thee, they will incite thee to sin, and if thou avoidest them, they will lay a snare for thee. So choose for thyself, and shun their society. I hold that the best counsel to-day is to dwell alone; for therein lies safety, and safety is a sufficient advantage.

The extreme pessimism of the outlook of Bishr is eloquently evidenced in verses attributed to him.[20]

> I swear it is the nobler part
> To drink the salt tears of the heart,
> And crush the datestone, than to stand
> With greed in soul, and cap in hand,
> To gain—for recompense enow!—
> The lowering glance and wrinkled brow.
> Then with despair be satisfied;
> 'Tis greater wealth than aught beside,
> A bargain to rejoice the soul.
> Despair is fine and worshipful;
> God's fear is true nobility,
> Desire leads on to infamy;
> For, let the world be fair to-day,
> It shall at last assault, and slay.

Meanwhile in Iraq the ascetic movement was similarly striking out in new directions. The violence of Bishr b. al-Hārith's reaction against society is fully matched by the sentiments of al-Fudail b. 'Iyād (d.187/803), himself a Khorasanian by birth who lived for many years at Kufa and died in Mecca. "In truth," he said, "I would rather be this dust, or this wall, than dwell in the shambles of the noblest of earth's inhabitants to-day. Thou fearest death; but dost thou know death? If thou tellest me that thou fearest death, I will not believe thee; for if thou didst indeed fear death, it would not profit thee to eat or to drink, or to possess anything in this world. If thou hadst known death truly, thou wouldst never have married, or desired children."[21]

A pupil remarks that he accompanied al-Fudail for thirty years and never saw him laugh or smile except once, on the day his son 'Alī died; asking him the reason for this unexpected change of mood, he received the answer, "Almighty God desired a certain thing, and I desired what God desired."[22]

A less lugubrious though equally austere note is struck in the utterances of Rābi'a, the famous woman mystic of Basra (d.185/801). Her hand was sought in marriage by a number of pious men, but she declined all offers, declaring, "The contract of marriage is for those who have a phenomenal existence. But in my case, there is no such existence, for I have ceased to exist and have passed out of self. I exist in God and am altogether His. I live in the shadow of His command. The marriage contract must be asked for from Him, not from me."[23] Rābi'a was overwhelmed by the consciousness of the near presence of God; once, when ill, she said to a visitor who asked her what her sickness might be, "By God, I know of no cause for my illness, except that Paradise was displayed to me, and I yearned after it in my heart; and I think that my Lord was jealous for me, and so reproached me; and only He can make me happy."[24] Close to this saying is the mood of her celebrated prayer: "O God! if I worship Thee in fear of Hell, burn me in Hell; and if I worship Thee in hope of Paradise, exclude me from Paradise; but if I worship Thee for Thine own sake, withhold not Thine Everlasting

Beauty!"[25] With her name is generally associated the first enunciation in Sufism of the doctrine of Divine Love, which later came to be so dominant a feature of the movement: her short poem on this theme is one of the most often quoted in Sufi literature.

> Two ways I love Thee: selfishly,
> And next, as worthy is of Thee.
> 'Tis selfish love that I do naught
> Save think on Thee with every thought.
> 'Tis purest love when Thou dost raise
> The veil to my adoring gaze.
> Not mine the praise in that or this:
> Thine is the praise in both, I wis.[26]

We quoted at the beginning of this chapter some verses by Ahmad b. 'Āsim of Antioch, and will end our brief review of the early ascetics with him, for he furnishes an excellent example of the beginning of a transition which from his time forward gradually affected the character of Sufism; converting it from a way of life taken up as a protest against the worldliness prevalent in high places, into a theory of existence and a system of theosophy. Himself a pupil of a noted ascetic, Abū Sulaimān al-Dārānī, he is the writer of the earliest surviving treatises that can be truly said to be mystical in character, and he is thus the forerunner of the great Sufi authors of the third/ninth century.[27] A brief dialogue between him and an unnamed disciple shews him in the part of spiritual preceptor, a feature of Sufism which now assumes increasing importance.[28]

Q. What sayest thou of consulting with others?
A. Have no faith in it, save it be with a trustworthy man.
Q. And what sayest thou concerning the giving of advice?
A. Consider first whether thy words will save thyself; if so, thy guidance is inspired, and thou wilt be respected and trusted.

Q. What thinkest thou of association with other men?

A. If thou findest an intelligent and trustworthy man, associate with him, and flee from the rest as from wild beasts.

Q. How may I best seek to draw near to God?

A. By leaving the inward sins.

Q. Why inward rather than outward?

A. Because if thou avoidest inward sins, the outward sins will be void as well as the inward.

Q. What is the most harmful sin?

A. The sin thou dost not know to be a sin. And more harmful than this is to suppose that it is a virtuous act, while all the time it is a sin.

Q. What sin is the most profitable to me?

A. The sin thou keepest before thine eyes, weeping over it constantly until thou departest from the world, so that thou wilt never have committed the like again. That is 'sincere repentance' (cf. Kor. 66:8).

Q. What is the most harmful virtuous act?

A. The kind that causes thee to forget thy evil deeds; the kind thou keepest before thine eyes, relying upon it and confident, so that in thy delusion thou fearest not for the evil thou hast done, on account of pride.

Q. Where is my person most concealed?

A. In thy cell, and within thy house.

Q. And if I am not safe in my house?

A. In any place where lusts do not cleave to thee, and temptations do not beset thee.

Q. What grace of God is most profitable to me?

A. When He protects thee from disobeying Him, and assists thee to obey Him.

Q. This is a summary: explain it to me more clearly.

A. Very well. When He assists thee with three things: a reason that suffices thee against the vexation of thy passion, a knowledge that suffices thee for thy ignorance, and a self-sufficiency that drives away from thee the fear of poverty."

FIVE

THE MYSTICS

> Thereafter the first did not fail to call the second, and
> the predecessor the successor, with the tongue of his work,
> which freed him of the necessity of speech. But then desire
> diminished and purpose flagged: and with this came
> the spate of questions and answers, books and treatises;
> the inner meanings were known to those who wrote, and
> the breasts of those who read were receptive to under-
> stand them.[1]

Arabia, Iraq, Syria and Khorasan had participated
equally in the growth of the ascetic movement. We have
watched self-denial (*zuhd*), a virtue applauded by the
most orthodox of Muslim theologians—and the illustrious
Ahmad b. Hanbal (d.241/855), founder of the strictest of
the four schools of Sunni jurisprudence, himself wrote a
book entitled *Kitāb al-Zuhd*[2]—gradually turning into
something quite different: a total disregard of worldly
wealth and ambition is exalted into an entire absorption
with the fear, and then the service, and finally the love of
God.

Asceticism for its own sake tends to become a rather
joyless and negative attitude to the universe; when warmed
by spiritual emotion it converts into an ardent fervour
rejoicing in hardship and delighting in ecstatic experience;
subjected to the searching light of speculative reason, it is
transformed into the hard discipline that is the necessary
prelude to a proved theosophy. This final development
took place at Baghdad, which now became the most
important centre of Sufism as it had also come to be the
focus of literature, theology, law and philosophy. No

doubt the free debates between Christians and Muslims, which for a brief period of splendid tolerance enlivened the Abbasid court, and the translation of Plato, Aristotle and the later Greek philosophers into Arabic, played an important part in stimulating this transition. The doctrine of the Divine Unity (*tauhīd*) exercised the minds of the learned and religious increasingly, as the contest between creeds and sects became keener; so that it is scarcely surprising that the Sufis should also have evolved their own interpretation of this crucial point in Islamic theology. But an examination of these interesting matters lies outside the scope which we have allowed ourselves in the present book.

The first Sufi author of the foremost rank whose preserved writings may truly be said to have formed to a large extent the pattern of all subsequent thought was al-Hārith b. Asad al-Muhāsibī. He was born at Basra in 165/781 but came early in life to Baghdad, where he passed the greater part of his days, dying in the Abbasid capital in 243/837. Being a keen student of *hadīth*, he lavished extreme care upon providing apostolic authority for his teachings; but Ahmad b. Hanbal condemned him for using "weak" traditionists, and he was constrained for a time to flee to Basra. One of his disciples was the eminent al-Junaid, who has supplied a revealing account of the relationship in which he stood to his master.[3]

> Al-Hārith b. Asad al-Muhāsibī used to come to my house and say, 'Come out with me, and let us grind.' I would say to him, 'Wilt thou drag me forth from my solitude and spiritual security into the highways and allurements, to behold lustful things?' He would answer, 'Come out with me: there is nothing for thee to fear.' And when I had come with him to a certain place where he sat down, he would say to me, 'Ask me a question.' I would reply, 'I have no question to ask thee.' Then he

would say, 'Ask me whatever comes into thy mind.'
Then the questions would rush upon me, and I would
question him, and he would answer accordingly forthwith;
then he would return to his dwelling-place and make them
into books.

Here we have the portrait of the Sufi teacher acting
like any other learned man of his time, composing his
fundamental works in reply to questions put to him by a
pupil. The structure of al-Muhāsibī's books, especially
his masterpiece al-Ri'āya li-huqūq Allah,[4] fully confirms
this description.

The bulk of al-Muhāsibī's writings is concerned with
self-discipline—his name is connected with the word for
self-examination (muhāsaba)—and al-Ri'āya in particular
exercised a great influence on the illustrious al-Ghazālī
(d.505/1111) when he came to write his Ihyā' 'ulūm al-dīn,
to which we shall refer later. His Kitāb al-Wasāyā (or
al-Nasā'ih) is a series of sermons mainly on ascetic themes.
The introduction to this work is autobiographical in
character, and may well have been in Ghazālī's mind
when the latter wrote his famous al-Munqidh min al-dalāl.
Some extracts translated from an unpublished manuscript
of the Wasāyā will indicate its character.

> It has come to pass in our days, that this community is
> divided into seventy and more sects: of these, one only is
> in the way of salvation, and for the rest, God knows best
> concerning them. Now I have not ceased, not so much as
> one moment of my life, to consider well the differences into
> which the community has fallen, and to search after the
> clear way and the true path, whereunto I have searched
> both theory and practise, and looked, for guidance on the
> road to the world to come, to the directing of the theolo-
> gians. Moreover, I have studied much of the doctrine of
> Almighty God, with the interpretation of the lawyers, and
> reflected upon the various conditions of the community,
> and considered its divers doctrines and sayings. Of all this

I understood as much as was appointed for me to understand: and I saw that their divergence was as it were a
deep sea, wherein many had been drowned, and but a
small band escaped therefrom; and I saw every party of
them asserting that salvation was to be found in following
them, and that he would perish who opposed them. Then
I considered the various orders of men. For some there
are who are acquainted with the nature of the world to
come, and do prefer it: such are hard to find, but they are
very precious. And some know nothing of this: to be far
from them is a boon. Some make show to be like them
that know, but are in love with the present world, and
prefer it. Some carry an uncertain knowledge of the other
world, but with that knowledge seek after respect and
elevation, obtaining through their otherworldliness
worldly goods. Some carry a knowledge, but know not the
interpretation of that knowledge. Some make a show to be
like the godly, and to resemble good folk, only they have
no strength in them: their knowledge lacks in penetration,
and their judgment cannot be trusted. Some possess
intellect and intelligence, but are lacking in piety and
goodness. Some secretly conform with their desires, being
ambitious for worldly gain, and seeking to be rulers of
men. Some are devils in human form: they turn their
faces from the world to come, and rush madly after this
world, greedy to collect it, avid of enrichment in it: report
says they live, but in truth they are dead; with them
virtue becomes an abomination, and evil-doing a virtue.
In all these classes of men I sought for my aim, but could
not find it. Then I sought out the guidance of them that
were right guided, looking for rectitude, truth and
guidance: I looked to knowledge for direction, thinking
deeply and considering long. Then it was made clear to
me, from God's Book, and the Prophet's practice, and
the consensus of believers, that the pursuit of desire blinds
to right direction, and leads astray from truth, causing one
to abide long in blindness. So I began to expel desire from
my heart. I paused before the divergences of the community, ardently seeking the party of salvation, and
anxiously avoiding fatal schisms and sects bound for
ruin; for I feared that I might die before finding the light.
With all my heart I sought for the path of salvation; and

I found, through the consensus of believers regarding the Revealed Book of God, that the path of salvation consists in laying hold of the fear of God, and performing His Ordinances, abstaining from what He has made lawful and unlawful alike and following all that He has prescribed, sincere obedience to God, and the imitation of His Prophet. So I sought to inform myself of God's Ordinances, and the Prophet's practices, as well as the pious conduct of the saints. I saw that there was both agreement and contrariety; but I found that all men were agreed that God's Ordinances and the Prophet's practices were to be found among those who, knowing God and knowing of God, laboured to win His Pleasure. I therefore sought from among the community men such as these, that I might follow in their footsteps and acquire knowledge from them; and I saw that they were exceedingly few, and that their knowledge was utterly swept away: as the Prophet said, 'Islam came a stranger, and shall return a stranger as it began.' Great then was my trouble, when I could not find godfearing men to be my guides; for I feared lest death should suddenly overtake me while my life was yet confused. I persevered in my quest for that which I must by all means know, not relaxing my caution nor falling short in counsel. Then the Merciful God gave me to know a people in whom I found my godfearing guides, models of piety, that preferred the world to come above this world. They ever counselled patience in hardship and adversity, acquiescence in fate, and gratitude for blessings received; they sought to win men to a love of God, reminding them of His Goodness and Kindness and urging them to repentance unto Him. These men have elaborated the nature of religious conduct, and have prescribed rules for piety, which are past my power to follow. I therefore knew that religious conduct and true piety are a sea wherein the like of me must needs drown, and which such as I can never explore. Then God opened unto me a knowledge in which both proof was clear and decision shone, and I had hopes that whoever should draw near to this knowledge and adopt it for his own would be saved. I therefore saw that it was necessary for me to adopt this knowledge, and to practise its ordinances; I believed in it in my heart, and embraced it in my mind, and made it the foundation of my faith. Upon this I have built my actions, in it moved in all my doings; and I ask God to quicken me to gratitude for His blessing me therewith, and to enable me to keep the Ordinances He has thereby taught me. Yet know I well my shortcoming in this, and that I can never thank my God for all that He has done for me.

The *Kitāb al-Taïwahhum* of al-Muhāsibī is a highly imaginative and artistic presentation of the terrors of death and the Last Judgment, culminating in a splendid picture of the Beatific Vision. But his most original thought is contained in a treatise on Love (*fasl fi 'l-mahabba*) which is only known to us by quotation; the extract which follows indicates something of its subtlety and originality.[6]

Q. And what is the Original Love?
A. The love of Faith; God has testified to the love of the faithful, saying, 'And those who believe do love God the stronger' (Kor. 2:160). The light of yearning is the light of love (*mahabba*); its superabundance is of the light of fondness (*widād*). Yearning is stirred up in the heart by the light of fondness. When God kindles that lamp in the heart of His servant, it burns fiercely in the crevices of his heart until he is lighted by it, and that lamp is never extinguished except when a man regards his actions with the eye of complacency. For if a man feels secure in his action from the malice of his adversary (Satan), he will parade that action without any trepidation of being deprived (of God's Grace); conceit thus occupies his heart; his soul runs wild in vainglory; and the Wrath of God descends upon him. It is just, if any man being entrusted by God with the charge of His Love delivers over the reins of his soul into the hands of complacency, that the loss (of God's grace) should bear him away swiftly to utter ruin. A pious woman once said, 'Ah! if only God had bestowed on those that yearn to meet Him such a state that, if they lost it, they would be deprived of ever-lasting bliss.' She was asked, 'And what might that state

be?' She replied, 'To regard their much (virtue) as little, and to wonder how it ever came to pass that their hearts should be the recipients of those (Divine) Favours.' A pious man was asked, 'Tell us about thy yearning for thy Lord—what does it weigh in thy heart?' He answered, 'Is this thing said to such as me? There is nothing in my heart that can be weighed, except in the presence of the soul; and if the soul is present while the heart is enjoying any heritage of proximity (to God), its joy is at once disturbed and turned to distress.' Mudar the Reader was asked, 'Which is better for the lover—fear or yearning?' He answered, 'This is a question I cannot answer; the soul has never looked upon anything without corrupting it.' 'Abd al-'Azīz b. 'Abd Allah recited to me these verses on the same subject.

> Best let the sinner grieve and fear,
> When he would turn to God in prayer;
> The heart obedient and pure
> Alone in Love may dwell secure;
> But they that noble are and wise
> Look unto God with yearning eyes.

For that reason it is said that love is yearning, because one does not yearn except for a beloved. There is no distinction between love and yearning, when yearning is a branch of the original love. It is said likewise that love is known by its evidences upon the bodies of the lovers, and in their speech, as also by the multitude of favours they enjoy through constant union with their Beloved. When God befriends them, He bestows His Favours upon them; and when these Favours become manifest, they are known for their love of God. Love itself has no manifesting shape or form, for its nature and form to be known; it is the lover who is known by his character, and the multitude of Favours which God displays upon his tongue, by gently guiding him, and by what is revealed to his heart. When the roots of these Favours are firmly established in the heart, the tongue speaks of the branches thereof; and God's Favours reach unto the hearts of those who love Him. The clearest sign of the love of God is excessive pallor, associated with continuous meditation, and prolonged

vigil accompanied by complete self-surrender, obediently
and with great haste ere dread death come upon him; and
the lover speaks of love according to the measure of the
Light bestowed upon him. Hence it is said, that the sign
of the love of God is the indwelling of God's Favours in the
hearts of those whom God has singled out for His Love.
A learned man quotes these lines on this theme.

> He hath His chosen few,
> Inspired to love Him true;
> Elect expressly so
> In ages long ago;
>
> Elect, or ever He
> Fashioned them forth to be
> The vessels of His Love,
> His Benefits to prove.

Contemporary with al-Muḥāsibī was Dhu 'l-Nūn the
Egyptian (d.246/861), whose tombstone at Giza still
survives. He is generally credited with having introduced
the idea of gnosis (maʿrifa) into Sufism, but this would
appear to be incorrect since the conception certainly
occurs in the fragments of earlier ascetics. Dhu 'l-Nūn is
represented in Sufi biographies as an almost legendary
figure, half-mystic half-alchemist; he is said to have known
the ancient Egyptian hieroglyphs, and to have been
familiar with the Hermetic wisdom. A number of short
treatises of extremely doubtful authenticity are attributed
to him; his poems and prayers, so much as are preserved
of them, give a truer impression of his mode of thought,
which is marked by distinctly pantheistic tendencies.

> O God, I never hearken to the voices of the beasts or
> the rustle of the trees, the splashing of waters or the song of
> birds, the whistling of the wind or the rumble of thunder,
> but I sense in them a testimony to Thy Unity (waḥdānīya),
> and a proof of Thy Incomparableness; that Thou art the
> All-prevailing, the All-knowing, the All-wise, the All-just,

the All-true, and that in Thee is neither overthrow nor
ignorance nor folly nor injustice nor lying. O God, I
acknowledge Thee in the proof of Thy handiwork and the
evidence of Thy acts: grant me, O God, to seek Thy
Satisfaction with my satisfaction, and the Delight of a
Father in His child, remembering Thee in my love for
Thee, with serene tranquillity and firm resolve.[7]

In his poetry Dhu 'l-Nūn uses the passionate language of
the devoted lover, as Rābi'a of Basra had done before him,
and so helped to fix a tradition that is thereafter so prominent a characteristic of Sufi literature.

> I die, and yet not dies in me
> The ardour of my love for Thee,
> Nor hath Thy Love, my only goal,
> Assuaged the fever of my soul.
>
> To Thee alone my spirit cries;
> In Thee my whole ambition lies,
> And still Thy Wealth is far above
> The poverty of my small love.
>
> I turn to Thee in my request,
> And seek in Thee my final rest;
> To Thee my loud lament is brought,
> Thou dwellest in my secret thought.
>
> However long my sickness be,
> This wearisome infirmity,
> Never to men will I declare
> The burden Thou hast made me bear.
>
> To Thee alone is manifest
> The heavy labour of my breast,
> Else never kin nor neighbours know
> The brimming measure of my woe.
>
> A fever burns below my heart
> And ravages my every part;
> It hath destroyed my strength and stay,
> And smouldered all my soul away.

Guidest Thou not upon the road
The rider wearied by his load,
Delivering from the steeps of death
The traveller as he wandereth?

Didst Thou not light a Beacon too
For them that found the Guidance true
But carried not within their hand
The faintest glimmer of its brand?

O then to me Thy Favour give
That, so attended, I may live,
And overwhelm with ease from Thee
The rigour of my poverty.[8]

Far bolder and more immoderate in the language of pantheism is Abū Yazīd (Bāyazīd) of Bistam, the Persian (d.261/875), first of the "intoxicated" Sufis who, transported upon the wings of mystical fervour, found God within his own soul and scandalised the orthodox by ejaculating, "Glory to Me! How great is My Majesty!" His ecstatic utterances (shathīyāt) were a grave embarrassment to his more "sober" brethren, until they developed the technique of interpreting them as innocent of the blasphemy that to the uninitiated seemed all too apparent in them; al-Junaid himself, a very lucid and subtle thinker and no "drunkard", exercised his ingenuity in writing a commentary upon them.[9] Abū Yazīd was also the first to take the Prophet's Ascension (mi'rāj) as a theme for expressing his own mystical experience, in this setting a fashion which others later followed.[10]

I saw that my spirit was borne to the lheavens. It looked at nothing and gave no heed, though Paradise and Hell were displayed to it, for it was freed of phenomena and veils. Then I became a bird, whose body was of Oneness and whose wings were of Everlastingness, and I continued to fly in the air of the Absolute, until I passed into the sphere of Purification, and gazed upon the field of

Eternity and beheld there the tree of Oneness. When I
looked I myself was all those. I cried: 'O Lord, with my
egoism I cannot attain to Thee, and I cannot escape from
my selfhood. What am I to do?' God spake: 'O Abū
Yazīd, thou must win release from thy thou-ness by following my Beloved (sc. Muhammad). Smear thine eyes with
the dust of his feet and follow him continually'.

Similar in spirit is another narrative attributed to Abū
Yazīd.[11]

> Once He raised me up and stationed me before Him,
> and said to me, 'O Abū Yazīd, truly My creation desire
> to see thee.' I said, 'Adorn me in Thy Unity, and clothe
> me in Thy Selfhood, and raise me up to Thy Oneness, so
> that when Thy creation see me they will say, We have
> seen Thee: and Thou wilt be That, and I shall not be
> there at all'.

Here we may observe fully developed the doctrine of
passing away in God (*fanā*) which from Abū Yazīd's
time onwards assumes a central position in the structure
of Sufi theory. It was after all not a difficult transition to
make from saying that all else but God is nothing (which
is the logical outcome of the extreme ascetic teaching that
the world is worthless and only God's service is a proper
preoccupation of the believer's heart), to claiming that
when self as well as the world has been cast aside the
mystic has passed away into God.

Credit for reconciling this daring but logical development with the orthodox doctrines of the Divine Unity
(*tauhīd*) is sometimes assigned to Ahmad b. 'Īsā al-
Kharrāz (d.286/899);[12] however, his *Kitāb al-Sidq*, which
alone survives of his writings, is pitched at a somewhat
lower level of thought. Nevertheless this little book is full
of interest and significance to the student of mysticism.
The author was at pains to prove that all the prophets of

old followed the kind of life which the Sufis sought to attain.[13] The climax of the treatise is an eloquent and, as it seems, authentic description of the state of intimacy with God.[14]

> Know that the disciple who is seeking after truthfulness acts in all his affairs in the fear of God, keeping watch over his heart, his purpose, and his members, and examining them. He concentrates his purpose, being afraid lest aught which concerns him not should enter into it, and being afraid of heedlessness, lest his bodily motions as manifested in his external members cause him to be somewhat wanting, and lest the purposes which enter inwardly into his heart perturb his (single) purpose. Thus he frees himself from all such motions, even if they be right and proper: for the heart is overwhelmed by an urgent desire that his recollection (of God) shall be perpetual, and his purpose single. If he continues thus, his heart gains a quick understanding, and his thoughts become clear, and light lodges in his heart: he draws near to God, and God overwhelms his heart and purpose. Then he speaks, and his heart surges with the recollection of God: the love of God lurks deeply hidden in his inmost heart, cleaving to his mind, and never leaving it. Then his soul is joyfully busied with secret converse with God, and passionate study, and ardent talk. So he is, eating and drinking, sleeping (and waking), in all his motions: for when God's nearness takes possession of a man's heart, it overwhelms all else, both the inward infiltrations of the purposes and the outward motions of the members. Thereafter that man continues, going or coming, taking or giving: there prevails in him the purpose which has ruled his mind, namely, the love of God and His nearness.

So far as reliable documentation goes, it appears that the responsibility for developing the doctrine of *fanā'* as an integral part of a well-coordinated theosophy belongs to al-Junaid of Baghdad (d.298/910), pupil of al-Muhāsibī, called in later times "the Shaikh of the Order," by far the most original and penetrating intellect among the Sufis of his time. Whereas others before him and his contemporaries had by brilliant flashes of intuition grasped one or another of the spiritual heights now falling to their mastery, he, standing as it were upon the supreme mountain-peak of analytical thought, took within his ranging vision the whole landscape of mystical speculation stretching below him, and with an artist's eye brought it to comprehension and unity upon a single canvas. In a series of letters and brief tracts brought but recently to light,[15] he sketches in profoundly subtle, deeply meditated language a consistent system of Islamic theosophy which has certainly not been improved upon, and which formed the nucleus of all subsequent elaboration.

The classic definition of *tauhīd* given by al-Junaid, and quoted by many later writers, is that it consists in "the separation of the Eternal from that which was originated in time."[16] Taking as his point of departure the pre-eternal covenant sworn by man with God and referred to (according to Sufi exegesis) in the Koran,[17] he views the entire course of history as the quest of man to fulfil that covenant and return to "the state in which he was before he was." In a comment on the conversation said to have taken place between man and God on that remote occasion, al-Junaid writes:[18] "In this verse God tells you that He spoke to them at a time when they (sc. Adam's descendants) did not exist, except so far as they existed in Him. This existence is not the same type of existence as is usually attributed to God's creatures; it is a type of existence which only God knows and only He is aware of. God knows their existence; embracing them He sees them in the beginning when they are non-existent and unaware of their future existence in this world. The existence of these is timeless." Elsewhere he remarks: "In this verse God has stated that He spoke to them when they had no formal existence. This is possible because God perceives them in their spiritual existence. This spiritual existence connotes their knowledge of God spiritually without in any way postulating their being aware of their own individuality."

Man's separate and individual existence in the universe, according to al-Junaid, is the consequence of a deliberate act of God's Will, Who at the same time desires to "overcome" man's existence by the outpouring of His own Being. Commenting on the well known *hadīth*, "When I love him, I am his ear, so that he hears by Me, etc."[19], he remarks, "Then it is God Who strengthens him, Who enables him to achieve this, Who guides him and gives him the vision of what He wishes in the manner He wishes, so that he achieves rightness and is in accord with Truth. This then is the Act of God in him, the Gift of God to him and only to him. It is not to be attributed positively to the worshipper, since it does not originate from him."

In a definition he describes Sufism (*tasauwuf*) as meaning that "God should cause thee to die from thyself and to live in Him."[20] This "dying-to-self" is called by al-Junaid *fanā'* (a term reminiscent of the Koranic phrase "Every thing is perishing (*fānin*) except His Face"[21]; the "life-in-Him" is named *baqā'* (continuance). By passing away from self the mystic does not cease to exist, in the true sense of existence, as an individual; rather his individuality, which is an inalienable gift from God, is perfected, transmuted and eternalised through God and in God. At the same time the return to continued existence is a source of trial (*balā'*) and affliction, for man is still apart and veiled from God; and so al-Junaid uses the imagery of the lover yearning after the Beloved, yet taking intense joy in the suffering which this separation causes him. Having enjoyed mystically anew the experience of life-in-God, and being restored to material life—"after their union with Him, He separates them from Himself (and grants them their individuality again), for He makes them absent (from this world) when they are in union with Him, and makes them present (in this world) when He has separated them from Himself"—thereafter "the souls of those who have known God seek after the verdant pastures, the beautiful vistas, the fresh green gardens" and every lovely thing in this physical world, to console them, as examples of God's handiwork, for the loss of the Artist's own Presence. It is to this dual sense of union and separation that al-Junaid refers in a short poem.[22]

> Now I have known, O Lord,
> What lies within my heart;
> In secret, from the world apart,
> My tongue hath talked with my Adored.
>
> So in a manner we
> United are, and One;
> Yet otherwise disunion
> Is our estate eternally.
>
> Though from my gaze profound
> Deep awe hath hid Thy Face,
> In wondrous and ecstatic Grace
> I feel Thee touch my inmost ground.

When al-Junaid in this way was succeeding to escape from the mortal peril of preaching the apotheosis of man, his junior contemporary al-Hallāj was not so fortunate in his reading of the riddle of existence, and being condemned for blasphemy he was executed upon the cross in 309/922. He went along with al-Junaid so far as seeing in the supreme mystical experience a reunion with God; but he then proceeded further and taught that man may thus be viewed as very God Incarnate, taking as his example not, as one might suppose, Muhammad, but Jesus. He did not claim Divinity for himself, though the utterance which led to his execution, "I am the Truth" (*ana 'l-haqq*)

seemed to his judges to have that implication. The
context of this startling paradox occurs in his *Kitāb
al-Tawāsīn*.[23]

> If ye do not recognise God, at least recognise His
> signs. I am that sign, I am the Creative Truth (*ana
> 'l-haqq*), because through the Truth I am a truth eternally.
> My friends and teachers are Iblis and Pharaoh. Iblis was
> threatened with Hell-fire, yet he did not recant. Pharaoh
> was drowned in the sea, yet he did not recant, for he would
> not acknowledge anything between him and God. And I,
> though I am killed and crucified, and though my hands
> and feet are cut off—I do not recant.

In al-Hallāj we have the supreme example—even
more extreme than Abū Yazīd—of the "intoxicated" Sufi;
so complete was his absorption in serving the Will of God
as he conceived it to be that he was utterly reckless of the
consequences, which in his case were certainly disastrous.
The legend of his death invests him with extraordinary
nobility, and challenges comparison with the Christian
story of the Crucifixion which may well have been in his
mind as his torturers made ready to slay him.

> When he was brought to be crucified and saw the
> cross and the nails, he turned to the people and uttered a
> prayer, ending with the words: 'And these Thy servants
> who are gathered to slay me, in zeal for Thy religion and
> in desire to win Thy favour, forgive them, O Lord, and have
> mercy upon them; for verily if Thou hadst revealed to
> them that which Thou hast revealed to me, they would
> not have done what they have done; and if Thou hadst
> hidden from me that which Thou hast hidden from them,
> I should not have suffered this tribulation. Glory unto
> Thee in whatsoever Thou doest, and glory unto Thee in
> whatsoever Thou willest'.[24]

The century which produced al-Muhāsibī, al-Junaid
and al-Hallāj abounded in Sufis of only comparatively

less significance, each of whom made his special contribution to building up the structure of Islamic mysticism. Not least important of these was al-Hākim al-Tirmidhī (fl. 280/893), the psychologist of Sufism, whose lost work the *Khatm al-wilāya* in which he argued that the saints had a "Seal" as well as the prophets compelled him to flee for his life, and was afterwards a source of Ibn 'Arabī's theory of sainthood and prophetship.[25] In a review of this kind, however, it is impossible to include more than a brief account of the leading figures, and we conclude the present chapter by quoting a few verses of Yahyā b. Mu'ādh of Raiy in Persia (d. 258/871), the associate of Abū Yazīd, and of Abu 'l-Husain al-Nūrī of Baghdad (d.295/907), al-Junaid's colleague.

In doing so, we must draw attention to the important part played by mystical verse in the Sufi life. Many anecdotes of the early Sufis relate how fond they were of quoting love-poetry, often in the first place of a purely human character, which they interpreted allegorically to accord with their own passionate spiritualism. We have seen how such saints as Rābi'a and Dhu'l-Nūn composed original verse, sometimes of high quality, in which they expressed their emotions in frankly erotic imagery. Fully to understand the later poetry of Sufism, especially that of the Persian school—though this is equally characteristic of writers like Ibn al-Fārid and Ibn 'Arabī—it is necessary to keep in mind how fundamental in Sufi thought is this allegory of love, and how readily in their minds human and Divine imagery is interchanged.

Yahyā b. Mu'ādh writes:

> The lover joys to dwell
> In love with Love;
> Yet some, as strange I tell,
> Do Love reprove,

> About God's Love I hover
> While I have breath,
> To be His perfect lover ·
> Until my death.[26]

In another short poem he gives us an interesting glimpse of the Sufi ritual of dancing, which had already so early begun to enliven their austerities and was later to become an essential feature of their spiritual life.[27]

> The Truth we have not found;
> So, dancing, we beat the ground;
> Is dancing reproved in me
> Who wander distraught for Thee?
> In Thy valley we go around,
> And therefore we beat the ground.

A man came to Abu 'l-Husain al-Nūrī on the eve of the Bairam festival, and asked him what garments he proposed to wear upon the morrow. He answered:[28]

> 'To-morrow is the festival!' they cried,
> 'What robe wilt thou put on?' And I replied:
> 'The robe He gave me, Who hath poured for me
> Full many a bitter potion. Poverty
> And Patience are my raiment, and they cover
> A heart that sees at every feast its Lover.
> Can there be finer garb to greet the Friend,
> Or visit Him, than that which He doth lend?
> When Thou, my Expectation, art not near,
> Each moment is an age of grief and fear;
> But while I may behold and hear Thee, all
> My days are glad, and Life's a Festival!'

On another occasion al-Nūrī declaimed:[29]

> So passionate my love is, I do yearn
>   To keep His memory constantly in mind;
> But O, the ecstasy with which I burn
>   Sears out my thoughts, and strikes my memory blind!

And, marvel upon marvel, ecstasy
    Itself is swept away: now far, now near
My Lover stands, and all the faculty
    Of memory is swept up in hope and fear.

The following verses, also attributed to al-Nūrī, come very close to expounding the doctrine which we have described as taught by al-Junaid. [30]

I had supposed that, having passed away
    From self in concentration, I should blaze
A path to Thee; but ah! no creature may
    Draw nigh Thee, save on Thy appointed ways.
I cannot longer live, Lord, without Thee;
Thy Hand is everywhere: I may not flee.

Some have desired through hope to come to Thee,
    And Thou hast wrought in them their high design:
Lo! I have severed every thought from me,
    And died to selfhood, that I might be Thine.
How long, my heart's Beloved? I am spent:
I can no more endure this banishment.

SIX

THE THEORISTS OF SUFISM

THE 4/10th century did not lack for individual creative thinkers in Sufism, such as al-Junaid's pupil Abū Bakr al-Shiblī of Baghdad (d.334/946), Abū Bakr al-Wāsitī of Farghana (d.331/942), Muhammad b. 'Abd al-Jabbār al-Niffarī (fl.350/961) and Ibn al-Khafīf of Shiraz (d.371/982). Of these the most curious and interesting figure is al-Niffarī, who left behind him a series of "revelations" (*Kitāb al-Mawāqif* and *Kitāb al-Mukhātabāt*[1]) purporting to have been received from God in a state of ecstasy, possibly by automatic writing. While these are for the most part brief sentences, composed in general in a highly technical vocabulary and style, and require a commentary to be understood, certain passages have an authentic beauty and seem to possess the ring of genuine mystical experience. The writer pictures himself as standing before God (*mauqif*—a term perhaps originally borrowed from the descriptions of the Last Day) in one or other spiritual state, and hearing God speaking to him. The pattern for this situation was no doubt borrowed from Abū Yazīd—we have quoted above an example pointing to this conclusion[2]—but the treatment is new.

He stayed me in Death; and I saw the acts, every one of them, to be evil. And I saw Fear holding sway over Hope; and I saw Riches turned to fire and cleaving to the fire; and I saw Poverty an adversary adducing proofs; and I saw every thing, that it had no power over any other thing; and I saw this world to be a delusion, and I saw the heavens to be a deception. And I cried out, 'O Knowledge!'; and it answered me not. Then I cried

64

out, 'O Gnosis!'; and it answered me not. And I saw every thing, that it had deserted me, and I saw every created thing, that it had fled from me; and I remained alone. And the act came to me, and I saw in it secret imagination, and the secret part was that which persisted; and naught availed me, save the Mercy of my Lord. And He said to me, 'Where is thy knowledge?' And I saw the Fire. And he said to me, 'Where is thy act?' and I saw the Fire. And He said to me, 'Where is thy gnosis?' And I saw the Fire. And He unveiled for me His Gnoses of Uniqueness, and the Fire died down. And He said to me, 'I am thy Friend.' And I was stablished. And He said to me, 'I am thy Gnosis.' And I spoke. And He said to me, 'I am thy Seeker.' And I went forth. [3]

But the age of al-Niffarī was above all a period of organisation and construction. The Persian Hujwīrī, writing in the middle of the 5/11th century, enumerates no fewer than twelve "sects" of Sufism, of which ten are stated to be "orthodox" and two "heretical"[4]; these "sects" are named with one exception after their reputed founders, and a body of distinctive doctrine is assigned to each. Hujwīrī's learned translator saw "no adequate ground at present" for supposing his author to be merely inventing for the sake of systematisation, though he adds, "It is very likely that in his account of the special doctrines which he attributes to the founder of each School he has often expressed his own views upon the subject at issue and has confused them with the original doctrine."[5] It is curious that no other writer but Hujwīrī supplies this information, however, and his evidence must of necessity be treated with suspicion; but we are on safe ground enough if we assume, as the general body of documentation justifies us in assuming, that the group of pupils which attended each great Sufi teacher preserved, and in turn transmitted to their pupils, as much as they remembered of their master's instruction, thus creating at least the illusion of forming, not indeed "sects," but well founded and individual "schools" of Sufi tradition. A fair parallel would be the chains of transmission which are found prefixed to many ancient Arabic manuscripts of books on various subjects, including Sufism.

During the 4/10th century this work of preserving and handing-on the teachings of the Sufi masters continued apace. What is more important and significant, we now for the first time meet with systematic and documented "histories" of Sufism—a sure sign that the task of building was felt to be complete and that the movement was now sufficiently established and organised to be capable of description and discussion. Another and certainly more urgent motive for undertaking this work was provided by the scandal which culminated in the execution of al-Hallāj. The Sufis had been under the fire of the narrowly orthodox for some considerable time, and scarcely any of their prominent teachers after al-Muhāsibī escaped the accusation of being *zindīq*—a convenient portmanteau term of abuse used by the zealots to cover a multitude of suspected heresies. There was thus an urgent need to rehabilitate the movement, if it was to survive in these less liberal times and continue to be an effective force in the community. The need produced the men, and the men produced the books eminently suitable for the purpose.

The first to address himself to this labour was Abū Sa'īd Ibn al-A'rābī, a learned jurist and Traditionist, a disciple of al-Junaid, who died at Mecca in 341/952 at the age of 94. His *Tabaqāt al-nussāk* ("Classes of the Pious," a term reminiscent of the *tabaqāt* of poets, lawyers, theologians, grammarians and other scholars which were being compiled at about the same time) has unfortunately not survived, but what we know of it by quotation makes it clear that the author gave a fairly full account of the lives and teachings of the great Sufi masters. We regret equally the loss of the *Hikāyāt al-auliyā'* ("Tales of the Saints") by Abū Muhammad al-Khuldī (d. 348/959), but happily it is extensively reproduced by later writers and so its contents have not wholly perished.

The oldest surviving general account of Sufism, and in many respects the most valuable, is the *Kitāb al-Luma'* of Abū Nasr al-Sarrāj (d. 378/988) [6]. This great and fundamental book, which is fortunately accessible in a sound edition and an English summary, differs in character from the biographical sketches of Ibn al-A'rābī and al-Khuldī as being constructed, more after the pattern of theological treatises, in such a fashion as to describe and analyse the doctrines and practices of the Sufis; the author also gives particular attention to the technical vocabulary of the movement, which had by his time become both copious and complex. One entire section is devoted to the "imitation of the Prophet," and another to accounts proving the saintliness of the Prophet's Companions; al-Sarrāj describes the miracles that have been accorded to the especially holy, and discusses the differences of doctrine dividing certain schools of Sufism. While he defends at length the "ecstatic utterances" (*shathīyāt*) of various mystics, and in particular those of Abū Yazīd whose interpretation by al-Junaid he quotes verbatim, he concludes his book with a long and detailed exposure of the "errors" of theory and practice committed by some Sufis. The *Kitab al-Luma'* is extraordinarily well documented, and abounds in quotations not only from the sayings and poems but also from the letters of the mystics; its author was living at no great distance from the golden age of al-Muhāsibī and al-Junaid, and gives the impression of being as honest as he is well-informed.

In al-Sarrāj we may recognise a thinker after al-Junaid's heart, a man more immediately concerned with the theosophy than with the discipline of Sufism. His con-

temporary Abū Tālib al-Makkī (d. 386/996) perhaps
reminds us rather of al-Muḥāsibī. He is well grounded in
theology and Traditions, and is greatly interested to
prove the orthodoxy of Sufi doctrine and practice, so that
his famous work, the *Qūt al-qulūb*, is found to contain
somewhat more of careful argument and somewhat less
of curious quotation. Nevertheless the book is of primary
importance, as being the first—and a very successful—
attempt to construct an overall design for orthodox
Sufism; like al-Muḥāsibī, Abū Tālib al-Makkī was carefully studied by al-Ghazālī and exercised considerable
influence on his mode of thought and writing. The
pattern of the *Qūt al-qulūb* is a little reminiscent of that of
the standard manuals of religious jurisprudence, with its
minute discussion of the ritual practices of Islam which
are, however, treated from the mystical standpoint. He is
by no means content to answer the criticisms of the
professional theologians but carries the war into the
enemy's camp. Claiming that the Sufi way of life and
thought represented an authentic tradition of the Prophet's
teaching, transmitted first by al-Hasan al-Basrī and
maintained scrupulously intact by relays of teachers and
disciples, he declares that the fashion of writing on
dogmatic theology was itself an innovation, and an evil
one at that[7].

> They used to receive the instruction one from the other
> and preserved it carefully, because their hearts were clear
> of doubts, free from worldly preoccupations, and unsullied
> by passion; because their purpose was lofty, their reso-
> lution strong, and their intention excellent. Then, after
> the year 200, and when three centuries had elapsed,
> in this deplorable fourth century the compilations on
> scholastic theology (*kalām*) first appeared, and the
> scholastic theologians began to write according to opinion,
> reason and analogy. Gone now was the instruction (*'ilm*)
> of the pious, vanished the intuitive knowledge (*ma'rifa*) of

the firm of faith—the teaching of piety, the inspiration of rectitude and belief. So matters have continued to develop down to this present time. Now the scholastic theologians are called learned (*'ulamā'*), the mere romancers are named gnostics (*'ārifīn*), the narrators and informants learned, though they have no true grounding in religious lore nor the apperception that comes of faith.

For all the care lavished by the author on avoiding extremist views, it is perhaps scarcely surprising that his work was not received with favour by strict Sunni opinion.

Towards the end of the century a third fundamental though much shorter treatise on Sufism was written by Abū Bakr al-Kalābādhī (d. 390/1000), who also composed a book on Traditions. His *al-Ta'arruf li-madhhab ahl al-tasauwuf*[8] is still more frankly apologetic than his predecessors' works had been. The author takes one by one the essential elements of Islamic theology, quoting as it seems verbally from the "creed" known as *al-Fiqh al-akbar* (II), and asserts of each in turn that it was firmly held by the great Sufis; he produces quotations to prove his points. After this task of rehabilitation has been completed, al-Kalābādhī sketches briefly and section by section the characteristic mystical doctrines of Sufism, and concludes his little handbook with some paragraphs on miracles. This manual was well regarded in later times; commentaries upon it were written by, among others, the celebrated Persian mystic Ansārī (d. 481/1088) and Qonawi (d. 729/1329), and it was extensively quoted by the Egyptian polymath Jalāl al-Dīn al-Suyūtī (d. 911/1505).

A little later than al-Kalābādhī wrote Abū 'Abd al-Rahmān al-Sulamī (d. 421/1021), a copious author who is best known for his biographies of Sufis, the *Tabaqāt al-Sūfīyīn*.[9] This rather short book, apart from its intrinsic value, is interesting chiefly as being the basis of Ansārī's

Tabaqāt al-Sūfīya, composed in the Persian dialect of Herat, which served in turn as the foundation upon which the illustrious poet Jāmī (d. 898/1944) constructed his *Nafahāt al-uns*. Perhaps more important, al-Sulamī also wrote a commentary on the Koran from the Sufi standpoint which has not yet been thoroughly studied but is likely to be extremely valuable, as shewing how the mystics addressed themselves to this, the fundamental Muslim science. A short treatise by the same author on the "errors of the Sufis" is our best source of information concerning the Malāmatīya,[10] an extremist sect who held that the true worship of God is best proved by the contempt in which the devotee is held by his fellow-men; on this argument they justified not only the total neglect of the religious prescriptions of Islam, but the commission of the most outrageous sins as testifying to their disregard of human opinion and judgment. This rather unsavoury development of "drunken" Sufism achieved wide notoriety in later times and brought the whole movement into disrepute.

The 5/11th century found Sufism firmly established and widespread throughout all Islam. Early in this period the distinguished historian Abū Nuʿaim al-Isbahānī (d. 430/1038) wrote what is unquestionably the most important and valuable work on Sufi biography and individual doctrine, the massive *Hilyat al-auliyā'*. This veritable encyclopaedia, which has been printed in ten volumes, takes into the category of "saints" not only a large number of the Companions of Muhammad and their followers—including the "righteous" caliphs—but also the four founders of the Sunni schools of jurisprudence. The bulk of the work is concerned with the ascetic rather than the theosophical side of Sufism, but the three concluding volumes, and especially the last two, are replete with the most careful documentation of mysticism in the ninth and tenth centuries.

While the *Hilyat al-auliyā'* is essentially a reference work and like all biographical dictionaries is deficient in construction, we possess in the celebrated *Risāla* of Abū 'l-Qāsim al-Qushairī (d. 465/1072) a carefully designed and admirably complete general account of the theoretical structure of Sufism. This medium sized work is the most esteemed and popular book on the subject in Arabic, and was the principal study of all later scholars, at a time when Sufism had come to be regarded as one of the Islamic "sciences"; commentaries were composed by several, including the learned Zakariyā' al-Ansārī of Cairo (d. 916/1511 or 926/1521). Like al-Sulamī, al-Qushairī also wrote a commentary on the Koran which has similarly not yet been studied, as well as numerous other books including a monograph on the Prophet's Ascension; but his fame chiefly and justly rests upon the *Risāla* which, as giving our most concise and authoritative description of Sufi doctrine, will be used in the next chapter where we shall present an outline of the mystical system as fully evolved and widely accepted from the 5/11th century onwards.

Almost contemporary with al-Qushairī is the earliest formal study of Sufism in Persian, the *Kashf al-mahjūb* of Hujwīrī (fl. 450/1057), from which we have quoted above; this important work, similar in pattern to the *Risāla* but with some remarkable individual features, is available in an excellent English translation and therefore requires no further description here.[11]

We conclude this sketch of the early theorists by referring to one other outstanding figure of the period, a man who was both a devout practising mystic and a theorist, the Persian 'Abd Allah al-Ansārī (d. 481/1088), better known in Persia by his poetical soubriquet Pīr-i Ansār. We have already mentioned him as the author of a biographical work on the Sufis in a Persian dialect;

equally famous is his very brief sketch in Arabic of Sufi theory, the *Manāzil al-sā'irīn*, which has been the subject of very many commentaries. He was a good poet in Persian, though not many of his poems have come down to us; he also composed in that language a number of devotional works of which the favourite is his *Munājāt* or orisons in a mixture of rhyming prose and verse[12]. The following translation of its opening passages, beginning with a *ghazal* (lyric) and ending with a *rubā'ī* (quatrain), will give an impression of the character of this charming little book.

Thou, Whose Breath is sweetest perfume to the spent and anguished heart,
Thy remembrance to Thy lovers bringeth ease for every smart.
Multitudes like Moses, reeling, cry to earth's remotest place:
"Give me sight, O Lord!' they clamour, seeking to behold Thy Face.
Multitudes no man has numbered, lovers, and afflicted all,
Stumbling on the way of anguish, 'Allah! Allah!' loudly call.
And the fire of separation sears the heart and burns the breast,
And their eyes are wet with weeping for a love that gives not rest.
'Poverty's my pride'—Thy lovers raise to heav'n their battle-cry,
Gladly meeting men's derision, letting all the world go by.
Such a fire of passion's potion Pir-i Ansar quaffing feels
That distraught, like Laila's lover, through a ruined world he reels.

O Generous, who Bounty givest!
O Wise, Who sins forgivest!
O Eternal, Who to our senses comest not near!
O One, Who art in Essence and Quality without peer!

O Powerful, Who of Godhead worthy art!
O Creator, who shewest the way to every erring heart!
To my soul give Thou of Thy Own Spotlessness,
And to my eyes of Thy Own Luminousness;
And unto us, of Thy Bounty and Goodness, whatever may
   be best
Make Thou that Thy Bequest.

O Lord, in Mercy grant my soul to live,
And patience grant, that hurt I may not grieve:
   How shall I know what thing is best to seek?
Thou only knowest: what Thou knowest, give!

This is the prototype of all the devotional literature in
Persian Sufism. Ansārī, with his senior contemporary
Abū Saʿīd b. Abi 'l-Khair (d. 440/1049), created the
pattern of thought and expression which afterwards
became universally famous in the writing of Sanāʾī,
ʿAttār, Rūmī, Saʿdī, Hāfiz, Jāmī and innumerable other
greater or lesser poets of Eastern Islam.

SEVEN

THE STRUCTURE OF SUFI THEORY AND PRACTICE

By the end of the 4/10th century Sufism had become a fairly rigid and clearly definable way of life and system of thought. When al-Qushairī wrote his *Risāla* ('Epistle to the Sufis') in 438/1046 he had several earlier compendia to draw upon, and in fact we find him quoting quite freely from the writings of al-Sarrāj and al-Sulamī. The classical formulation of Sufi doctrine on the mystical side has always been held by the Sufis to have been finally accomplished by al-Qushairī; its reconciliation and assimilation with orthodox Sunni theology and religious law was the work of the great Abū Hāmid al-Ghazālī (d. 505/1111), carried out by stages in a considerable number of relatively short books, and consolidated and consummated in the *Ihyā' 'ulūm al-dīn*, which was written between 492/1099 and 495/1102.

After a brief preface the *Risāla*, which was composed with the express purpose of rescuing Sufism from the ill-fame to which it had been exposed by the extravagant antinomianism of the Malāmatīya, begins with the assertion that Sufi doctrine in no way conflicts with orthodox theology. The author proceeds to illustrate and justify this claim in a series of brief biographies of prominent Sufis, beginning his list with Ibrāhīm b. Adham; before him, he argues, the term *zāhid* (abstainer) or *'ābid* (devotee) was applied to saintly men generally, but after the rise of schismatic sects the pious among the orthodox (Sunnis) were distinguished by the new title of Sufi.[1] The list of biographies concludes with the name of Abū 'Abd Allah al-Rūdhabārī (d. 369/980).

74

Next comes a section explaining certain technical terms current in Sufi literature. A fundamental distinction is drawn between *maqām* (station) and *hāl* (state); briefly, the *maqām* is a stage of spiritual attainment on the pilgrim's progress to God which is the result of the mystic's personal effort and endeavour, whereas the *hāl* is a spiritual mood depending not upon the mystic but upon God. "The states," says al-Qushairī, "are gifts; the stations are earnings."

The first station is stated to be conversion (*tauba*), a view commonly held by the Sufis[2], who mean by this term not of course the formal profession of Islam but the conscious resolve of the adult Muslim to abandon the worldly life and to devote himself to the service of God. It is in this sense, as we shall see, that al-Ghazālī after achieving a great reputation as a lawyer and a theologian turned away from formal religious learning and, experiencing conversion, declared himself to be a Sufi. Thereafter, al-Qushairī traces the penitent's onward journey according to the following pattern.

(2) *Mujāhada*, a collateral form of *jihād* (the so-called "holy war"), taken to mean "earnest striving after the mystical life." The term is based on the Koranic text, "And they that strive earnestly in Our cause, them We surely guide upon Our paths."[3] A Tradition makes the Prophet rank the "greater warfare" (*al-jihād al-akbar*) above the "lesser warfare" (*al-jihād al-asghar*, i.e. the war against infidelity), and explain the "greater warfare" as meaning "earnest striving with the carnal soul" (*mujāhadat al-nafs*).[4]

(3) *Khalwa wa-'uzla* (solitariness and withdrawal): the neophyte must train himself to live in isolation from his fellows, and so to rid himself of his evil habits.

(4) *Taqwā* (the awe of God), to strengthen the resolve and escape Divine chastisement.

(5) *Wara‘* (abstaining), that is, from all unnecessary and unseemly occupations.

(6) *Zuhd* (renunciation), even of permitted pleasures.

(7) *Samt* (silence): the Prophet is quoted as having said, "Whosoever believes in God and the Last Day, let him speak good, or else let him be silent." Silence is interpreted both literally, as meaning that a man should learn to govern his tongue, and metaphorically, as referring to a heart that silently accepts whatever God may decree.

(8) *Khauf* (fear), i.e. trepidation lest one's evil conduct may have unpleasant consequences in the future.

(9) *Rajā'* (hope), i.e. looking for a desired contingency in the future.

(10) *Huzn* (sorrow) for past sin.

(11) *Jū‘*, *tark al-shahwa* (hunger, denial of appetite), based on the Koranic text, "And We shall surely try you with somewhat of fear and hunger . . . And give glad tidings to them that are patient."[5]

(12) *Khushū‘*, *tawādu‘* (fearfulness, humility).

(13) *Mukhālafat al-nafs wa-dhikr ‘uyūbihā* (opposition to the carnal soul, remembering its vices): two vices are particularised, viz. (a) *hasad* (envy), (b) *ghība* (slander).

(14) *Qanā‘a* (contentment): the Prophet said, "Contentment is an imperishable treasure."

(15) *Tawakkul* (trust in God): God says, "Whoso trusteth in God, God sufficeth him."[6]

(16) *Shukr* (thankfulness): God says, "If ye are thankful, I will give you fuller measure."[7]

(17) *Yaqīn* (firm faith).

(18) *Sabr* (patience, fortitude).

(19) *Murāqaba* (constant awareness of God), as the Tradition says, "Righteousness consists in worshipping God as if thou seest Him; for if thou seest Him not, yet He sees thee."

(20) *Ridā* (satisfaction). This is accounted by some Sufis

to be the last of the "stations" and the first of the "states," in accordance with the Koranic text, "God was well-pleased with them, and they were well-pleased with God,"[8] which makes God's satisfaction with man a precondition of man's satisfaction with God.[9] According to al-Qushairī, the Khorasanian school held that *ridā* was a *maqām*, being a development out of *tawakkul*, whereas the Iraqi school maintained that it was a *hāl*: he mediates between the two views, taking the beginning of *ridā* to be a *maqām*, and its conclusion a *hāl*.

The final "station" is then followed by:—

(21) *'Ubūdīya* (servanthood), a true sense of being subject entirely to the Lord (*Rabb*) God.

(22) *Irāda* (desire), i.e. the desire to have no personal desire, only seeking what God desires.

(23) *Istiqāma* (uprightness), a "state" in which God's grace becomes perpetual, for it implies the perfect performance of God's service.

(24) *Ikhlās* (sincerity), that is, seeking only God in every act of obedience to Him.

(25) *Sidq* (truthfulness) in thought and act.

(26) *Hayā'* (shame), which the prophet declared to be "a part of faith (*īmān*)," a shame of being found wanting in sincerity.

(27) *Hurrīya* (magnanimity), the quality of being *hurr*, a "freeman," putting the interests of others before one's own, or of not being a "slave," sc. to material things.

(28) *Dhikr* (remembrance), having God constantly in mind and heart.

(29) *Futūwa* (chivalrousness), fulfilling the terms of the Tradition, "God will not fail to attend to His servant's need, so long as His servant attends to the needs of his Muslim brother," with complete self-disregard.

(30) *Firāsa* (insight), as the Prophet said, "Beware of the believer's insight, for he sees with the Light of God."

(31) *Khuluq* (moral character), the highest quality praised by God in His Prophet, saying, "Verily thou art (grounded) upon a noble (*'azīm*) character."[10]

(32) *Jūd, sakhā'* (generosity, bountifulness), for the Prophet said, "The bountiful man is near to God, near to men, near to Paradise, far from Hell."

(33) *Ghaira* (jealousy), in the sense of being jealous for God's service, not admitting any other thought into one's mind; it is an attribute of God Himself, Who is jealous lest His servant should commit any kind of sin.

(34) *Wilāya* (being in God's protection, sainthood), based on the Koranic text, "Verily God's proteges (*auliyā'*) have no cause to fear, neither do they grieve."[11]

(35) *Du'ā'* (prayer), being constantly suppliant to God, for God says, "Pray to Me, and I will answer you."[12]

(36) *Faqr* (poverty), for the Prophet said, "The poor shall enter Paradise five hundred years before the rich."

(37) *Tasauwuf* (purity), for al-Qushairī here prefers to derive this term from the root *ṣfw* (to be pure) rather than from *sūf* (wool).

(38) *Adab* (decent manners), as the Prophet said, "God mannered me, and taught me good manners," i.e. in religious conduct.

The foregoing (21-38) are all evidently extensions of the "stations" in al-Qushairī's view. After sections on (39) *safar* (travel), the merit and advantage of always being on the move rather than dwelling all one's life in one place, on (40) *suhba* (companionship), (41) *tauhīd* (true belief in One God), and (42) noble dying, he continues :—

(43) *Ma'rifa* (gnosis), which appears to mark the transition complete from "station" to "state," for this kind of knowledge comes into the heart from God when the mystic has stilled all the motions of his heart.

(44) *Mahabba* (love), a consequence of God's Love for man.[13]

(45) *Shauq* (yearning) to be constantly with God.

It will be seen that al-Qushairī, despite the care with which he analyses the mystic's moral and psychological advance, did not always mark carefully the distinction which later theorists observed between *maqām* and *ḥāl*. He differs even from his predecessor al-Sarrāj, who enumerated only seven stations (conversion, abstinence, renunciation, poverty, patience, trust in God, satisfaction) and ten states (meditation, nearness to God, love, fear, hope, longing, intimacy, tranquillity, contemplation, certainty).[14] But his analysis is otherwise clear and shrewd, and marks perhaps the highest point reached in this branch of Sufi theory.

Sufism had produced many men of conspicuous sincerity, holiness and intuition during the first four centuries of its existence; but it never made a more important conquest than when Abū Hāmid Muhammad b. Muhammad al-Ghazālī, the Hujjat al-Islām ("Proof of Islam"), declared himself its champion. Born in 451/1059 at Tus in Khorasan, al-Ghazālī lived his early years in this north Persian province which had raised up so many mystical geniuses. His schooling was that of an orthodox theologian and lawyer, and he had established himself as the leading Sunni scholar of his day when he was appointed professor of divinity at the Nizāmīya Madrasa, Baghdad, in 484/1091. Yet despite his celebrity and authority—his work as a lawyer in particular qualified him to be called the greatest Shāfi'ī jurisconsult after al-Shāfi'ī himself—he was dissatisfied with the intellectual and legalistic approach to religion, and felt a yearning for a more personal experience of God. In 488/1095 he gave up his teaching, and lived in retirement for ten years. The famous story of his conversion to Sufism is told in the autobiographical *al-Munqidh min al-dalāl*.[15]

Then I turned my attention to the Way of the Sufis. I knew that it could not be traversed to the end without both doctrine and practice, and that the gist of the doctrine lies in overcoming the appetites of the flesh and getting rid of its evil dispositions and vile qualities, so that the heart may be cleared of all but God; and the means of clearing it is *dhikr Allah*, i.e. commemoration of God and concentration of every thought upon Him. Now, the doctrine was easier to me than the practice, so I began by learning their doctrine from the books and sayings of their Shaykhs, until I acquired as much of their Way as it is possible to acquire by learning and hearing, and saw plainly that what is most peculiar to them cannot be learned, but can only be reached by immediate experience and ecstasy and inward transformation. I became convinced that I had now acquired all the knowledge of Sufism that could possibly be obtained by means of study; as for the rest, there was no way of coming to it except by leading the mystical life. I looked on myself as I then was. Worldly interests encompassed me on every side. Even my work as a teacher—the best thing I was engaged in—seemed unimportant and useless in view of the life hereafter. When I considered the intention of my teaching, I perceived that instead of doing it for God's sake alone I had no motive but the desire for glory and reputation. I realised that I stood on the edge of a precipice and would fall into Hellfire unless I set about to mend my ways . . . Conscious of my helplessness and having surrendered my will entirely, I took refuge with God as a man in sore trouble who has no resource left. God answered my prayer and made it easy for me to turn my back on reputation and wealth and wife and children and friends.

From his retirement until his death in 505/1111 al-Ghazālī lived the simple life of a mystic, punctuated only by study and the composition of a succession of books. In these he brought out various aspects of the moral, metaphysical and mystical system in which he essayed to reconcile Sufism with Muslim orthodoxy, and to prove that the Muslim life of devotion to the One God could not be lived perfectly save by following the Sufi way. While none of his shorter works is negligible, and some of especial value and importance, his masterpiece, and in many ways the greatest religious book composed by a Muslim, is the massive *Iḥyāʾ ʿulūm al-dīn* ('Revival of Religious Sciences').

A skeleton analysis of the contents of this famous treatise brings out its relationship on the one hand to orthodox theology and religious law, and on the other to practical and speculative mysticism. It is divided into four "quarters," each quarter being subdivided into a series of "books," in the following manner.

A. *Worship.*

(1) The Nature of Knowledge (*ʿilm*) ⎱ Epistemology and
(2) The Foundations of Belief ⎰ Theology
(3) The Inward Meaning of Purification ⎫
(4) The Inward Meaning of Prayer ⎪ Ritual and
(5) The Inward Meaning of Almsgiving ⎬ Canon Law
(6) The Inward Meaning of Pilgrimage ⎭
(7) On Reciting the Koran ⎫
(8) Recollections and Prayers ⎬ Devotional Works
(9) Orisons at Set Times ⎭

B. *Personal Behaviour.*

(1) Eating ⎫
(2) Drinking ⎪ Religious Law
(3) Earning ⎬
(4) Lawful and Unlawful Things ⎭
(5) Companionship ⎫
(6) Character ⎪
(7) Solitude ⎪
(8) Travel ⎬ Mystical
(9) Listening (to Music, Poetry), Ecstasy ⎪ Training
(10) Good Counselling ⎪
(11) Living and Prophetship ⎭

C. *The Deadly Sins.*

(1) The Wonderful Nature of the Heart
(2) Self-Discipline
(3) Gluttony and Sensuality
(4) Vices of Speech
(5) Anger, Malice and Envy — Psychology
(6) Worldly Goods — and Spiritual
(7) Wealth and Avarice — Discipline
(8) High Rank and Hypocrisy
(9) Arrogance and Conceit
(10) Pride

D. *The Way to Salvation.*

(1) Conversion (*tauba*)
(2) Fortitude (*sabr*) and Gratitude
    (*shukr*)
(3) Fear (*khauf*) and Hope (*rajā'*)
(4) Poverty (*faqr*) and Self-Denial
    (*zuhd*)
(5) Belief in One God (*tauhīd*) and Trust — Spiritual
    in God (*tawakkul*) — Experience
(6) Love (*mahabba*), Yearning (*shauq*),
    Intimacy (*uns*) and Satis-
    faction (*ridā*)
(7) Resolve (*nīya*), Truthfulness (*sidq*)
    and Sincerity (*ikhlās*)
(8) Contemplation (*murāqaba*) and Self-
    Examination (*muhāsaba*)
(9) Meditation (*tafakkur*) — Eschatology
(10) The Recollection of Death

A comparison has often been instituted between al-Ghazālī and St Augustine. "Ghazālī's conversion had for Islam consequences as important as St Augustine's conversion had for Christianity. This importance for Islam can be briefly characterised by saying that Ghazālī succeeded in assuring the mystical or introspective attitude a place within official Islam side by side with the legalism of the lawyers and the intellectualism of the theologians.''[16] By virtue of his profound learning in the accepted religious sciences, al-Ghazālī commanded the respect of all but the narrowest of the orthodox. His legal and theological training qualified him to bring to his constructive work on Sufism an intellect acute and sensitive, a mind ingenious and inventive. He had by heart all the terminology of the philosophers and the theologians. When to these intellectual gifts were added a theoretical knowledge and a personal experience of the Sufi life, al-Ghazālī was ready and able to perfect the work which Abū Tālib al-Makkī, al-Kalābādhī and al-Qushairī had all striven so hard to accomplish. Henceforward Sufism, at least of the "sober" type, was accepted as a Muslim science, and as a reasonable and laudable way of life.

EIGHT

THE SUFI ORDERS

THE mystical movement in Islam sprang, as we have seen, out of asceticism and was represented in its earliest phase by the personalities of individual men and women who, whether in town or desert—but especially in desert—devoted themselves singly and exclusively to the service of God and the joyous experience of His Grace. This period was followed by an age in which theory went hand in hand with practice, and famous shaikhs, themselves holy men, taught the nascent doctrine of Sufism to disciples, either solitary or in groups. The Persian theorist Hujwīrī, writing in the 5/11th century, enumerates several schools of mysticism which transmitted the teachings of the masters. The relation of teacher and pupil, familiar in other disciplines, presently developed into the characteristic Sufi counterpart of elder (*shaikh, pīr*) and disciple (*murīd, shāgird*); and convents (*ribāt, khānqāh*) were founded and endowed where a celebrated saint would reside with a group of his followers, who studied under him and worshipped with him for a shorter or a longer period. Initiation into the Sufi mysteries was marked by the investiture of a special frock (*khirqa*) symbolising his acceptance of and into a tradition of Divine service mounting back stage by stage to the Prophet Muhammad. So, Abū Saʿīd b. Abi ʾl-Khair (b.357/967) received his *khirqa* successively from al-Sulamī and Abu ʾl-ʿAbbās al-Qassāb.[1] It is important to remark that residence in a Sufi convent by no means implied celibacy, and most of the famous Muslim mystics are known to have been

84

married. So they interpreted the Tradition ascribed to Muhammad, "No monkery (*rahbānīya*) in Islam."

With the 6/12th century comes the foundation of the great Sufi Orders (*tarīqa*, lit. 'way'). Hitherto the convents had been isolated oases in the desert of worldly life; the time had come for them to be linked up in a widespread brotherhood of mystics acknowledging a common master and using a common discipline and ritual. The first of these Orders was the creation of Muhyī al-Dīn 'Abd al-Qādir b. 'Abd Allah al-Jīlī (al-Jīlānī). Born at Gilan in Persia in the year 471/1078, 'Abd al-Qādir migrated to Baghdad at the age of seventeen to study Hanbalī jurisprudence. Experiencing conversion, he began in 521/1127 to preach regularly on the holy life; many flocked to hear his sermons, attracted by the reports of the miracles he was said to perform. By his death in 561/1166 his influence had become so great that convents in many centres recognised his authority, and Sufis called themselves Qādirīs after his name. Many of 'Abd al-Qādir's writings, sermons and prayers have been preserved; his most celebrated book, *al-Ghunya li-tālibī tarīq al-haqq*, was for many generations a favourite manual of instruction. The Qādirī Order found followers in numerous parts of Islam, and was especially powerful in India, where its influence is widespread to the present day. No doubt a determining factor in the success of this and other similar Orders was their faithful adherence to the religious laws and practices of orthodoxy, and their strong condemnation of antinomianism and incarnationist tendencies. The *Ghunya* contains very little that could possibly be condemned by any but the most extreme "puritans"; its teaching is firmly based on the Koran and Traditions; the religious exercises it recommends are unobjectionable.

The second great Order to be constituted was the Suhrawardīya, so named after Shihāb al-Dīn 'Umar b.

'Abd Allah al-Suhrawardī (539-632/1144-1234), the youngest of three celebrated mystics bearing the same place-name. His uncle Abū Najīb (d.563/1168) was for a time Rector of the Nizāmīya Academy, and was a sound authority on Hadīth, which he taught to Shihāb al-Dīn; he also composed a small work on Sufism for beginners, the *Ādāb al-murīdīn*. His fellow-townsman Abu 'l-Futūh (d.587/1191) was a voluminous and imaginative writer of a characteristic Persian type, and being inclined towards pantheistic allegory he was condemned to death and executed for heresy. Shihāb al-Dīn was more fortunate; a model of orthodox moderation, he enjoyed the confidence and patronage of caliphs and princes, while his lectures and sermons were attended by admiring multitudes, many coming from far to hear him preach. Pilgrim to Mecca in 628/1231, he there met the great Egyptian mystic poet 'Umar b. al-Fārid; he numbered among his students the even more celebrated Persian poet Sa'dī (d.691/1292). Shihāb al-Dīn wrote many books large and small, the most famous and influential being the *'Awārif al-ma'ārif* which became the fundamental textbook of the Order. His teaching was carried to India by Bahā' al-Dīn Zakariyā' of Multan, and there found immediate acceptance. The name Suhrawardy is renowned in modern Bengal and Eastern Pakistani politics.

The third Order in date of creation owed its inspiration to a scholar of the Maghrib (Western Islam), Nūr al-Dīn Ahmad b. 'Abd Allah al-Shādhilī (593-656/1196-1258). A pupil of Ibn Mashīsh (d.625/1228), al-Shādhilī won such a large following in Tunis that the authorities feared his influence, and he found it more prudent to flee to Alexandria. His success in Egypt was prompt and astounding; the discipline and ritual which he taught crystallised into a distinctive Order which called itself after him. The Shādhilīya proved especially successful in

Egypt and North Africa generally, as well as in Arabia, Syria and elsewhere. The prayers (*ahzāb*, sing. *hizb*) of al-Shādhilī have been preserved and are used to this day in the devotions of his followers. A very influential member of the Order was Ibn 'Atā' Allah of Alexandria (d.709/1309), whose little collection of Sufi aphorisms, *al-Hikam al-'Atā'iya*, achieved an extraordinary popularity, as witness the large number of commentaries written upon it; in style and contents this work recalls the utterances of the Baghdad mystics of the ninth century. In the following specimens the parts in brackets represent the interpretation of the commentators.

A sign of relying upon (the efficacy of religious) performance (such as prayer and the like instead of upon God) is the diminishing of hope (for God's forgiveness) when slips (such as disobedience to the Divine Will) occur.

Thy desire to be isolated (from worldly things and to be only with God) when God causes thee to dwell in (secondary) causes comes of secret lust (after personal glory); and thy desire for (the possession of secondary) causes while God causes thee to dwell in isolation (therefrom) is a declension from the high purpose (to be united with God).

The (operations of the human) will controlling (the course of phenomena) do not pierce the walls of the (appointed) destinies (but are themselves merely a result of the Divine Will).

Give thyself rest from (attempting) the control (of human affairs), and what Another (sc. God) than thou has undertaken (to perform), do not undertake for thyself.

Thy labouring after (procuring for thyself) what He has guaranteed thee, and thy failure (to fulfil) what He has demanded of thee, is a proof of the blindness of thy (spiritual) vision.

Let not the postponement of the term of (God's) giving, despite (thy) importunity in praying (to Him), cause

thee to despair; for He has guaranteed to answer thee (in
what thou askest) according to how He chooses for thee,
not as thou choosest for thyself, and in the time He wills,
not in the time thou willest.

This attractive and eloquent little book, which has not
yet been translated, ends with a series of moving petitions
quite reminiscent of the *Munājāt* of Ansārī.

O God, seek me out of Thy Mercy that I may come to
Thee; and draw me on with Thy Grace that I may turn
to Thee.

O God, I shall never lose all hope of Thee even though
I disobey Thee; and I shall never cease to fear Thee
even though I obey Thee.

O God, the very worlds have themselves driven me
unto Thee, and my knowledge of Thy Bounty has brought
me to stand before Thee.

O God, how shall I be disappointed seeing that Thou
art my hope; or how shall I be despised seeing that in
Thee is my trust?

O Thou Who art veiled in the shrouds of Thy Glory,
so that no eye can perceive Thee! O Thou Who shinest
forth in the perfection of Thy Splendour, so that the
hearts (of the mystics) have realised Thy Majesty! How
shalt Thou be hidden, seeing that Thou art ever Manifest;
or how shalt Thou be absent, seeing that Thou art ever
Present, and watchest over us?

The fourth of the great Orders dating from this period
originated in Turkey and looks for founder to Jalāl al-Dīn
Rūmī (d.672/1273), called Maulānā, the greatest mystical
poet of Persia, of whom we shall be speaking subsequently;
it is entitled Maulawīya after him—the Turkish spelling
Mevleviya is perhaps more familiar. This Order achieved
paramount influence in Turkey under the Ottomans and
wielded great political power; its monasteries were
scattered throughout the Ottoman dominions. The most
characteristic feature of the Mevlevi ritual is the cele-

brated Whirling Dance, described by a number of European travellers who have witnessed it.

Many other Orders, either original foundations or their schismatic offshoots, sprang up throughout the Muslim world in the succeeding generations; they are now numbered in their hundreds, and their adherents counted in many millions. All have followed a broadly similar pattern. The Order is presided over in each age by the "successor" (*khalīfa*) of the founder, and his supremacy is acknowledged by the heads of the several branches in different centres. A relatively small number of professional Sufis reside in the lodges established for teaching and worship; the preponderant majority of adherents to the Orders are lay brethren, fully engaged in their mundane occupations, who prove their support by attending the ritual performances on the proper occasions.

Each Order is marked by its particular ritual, far more than by any discrimination of doctrine. E. W. Lane, who was in Egypt early last century at a time when the influence of the Orders was at its height and life in general had been little affected by modern thought or Western influence, gives us in his *Manners and Customs of the Modern Egyptians* some entertaining details of Sufi performances which he observed. These ceremonies, called *dhikr* (zikr in Lane's spelling which reflects the Egyptian dialect pronunciation)—the term originally means "remembrance" of God—have as their purpose, apart from their devotional aspect, the procuring of ecstatic experience; they are incidentally quite pleasant social occasions, and serve to knit together the heterogeneous elements attending them. I have myself been present at performances in which soldiers, policemen and tramdrivers in their uniforms partook side by side with workmen, porters, shopkeepers, clerks and the indeterminate multitude of a great city. The following is Lane's description of a Mevlevi performance. [2]

Most of the durweeshes were Egyptians; but there were among them many Turks and Persians. I had not waited many minutes before they began their exercises. Several of them first drove back the surrounding crowd with sticks; but as no stick was raised at me, I did not retire as far as I ought to have done; and before I was aware of what the durweeshes were about to do, forty of them, with extended arms, and joined hands, had formed a large ring, in which I found myself enclosed. For a moment I felt half inclined to remain where I was, and join in the zikr; bow, and repeat the name of God; but another moment's reflection on the absurdity of the performance, and the risk of my being discovered to be no durweesh, decided me otherwise; so, parting the hands of two of the durweeshes, I passed outside the ring. The durweeshes who formed the large ring (which enclosed four of the marble columns of the portico) now commenced their zikr; exclaiming over and over again, "Allah!" and, at each exclamation, bowing the head and body, and taking a step to the right; so that the whole ring moved rapidly round. As soon as they commenced this exercise, another durweesh, a Turk, of the order of Mowlawees, in the middle of the circle, began to whirl; using both his feet to effect this motion, and extending his arms: the motion increased in velocity until his dress spread out like an umbrella. He continued whirling thus for about ten minutes; after which he bowed to his superior, who stood within the great ring; and then, without showing any signs of fatigue or giddiness, joined the durweeshes in the great ring; who had now begun to ejaculate the name of God with greater vehemence, and to jump to the right, instead of stepping. After whirling, six other durweeshes, within the great ring, formed another ring; but a very small one; each placing his arms upon the shoulders of those next him; and thus disposed, they performed a revolution similar to that of the larger ring, except in being much more rapid; repeating, also, the same exclamation of 'Allah!' but with a rapidity proportionately greater. This motion they maintained for about the same length of time that the whirling of the single durweesh before had occupied; after which, the whole party sat down to rest. They rose again after the lapse of about a quarter of an hour; and performed the same exercises a second time.

In another place Lane gives an account of the so-called Doseh ceremony, performed by the "Saadeeyeh" Sufis, in which the Head of the Order rode on horseback over the prone devotees.[3] This done,

> He rode into the garden, and entered the house, of the Sheykh El-Bekree,[4] accompanied by only a few dur-weeshes. On my presenting myself at the door, a servant admitted me; and I joined the assembly within. The sheykh, having dismounted, seated himself on a seggadeh[5] spread upon the pavement against the end-wall of a tukhtabosh (or wide recess) of the court of the house. He sat with bended back, and down-cast countenance, and tears in his eyes; muttering almost incessantly. I stood almost close to him. Eight other persons sat with him. The durweeshes who had entered with him, who were about twenty in number, stood in the form of a semicircle before him, upon some matting placed for them; and around them were about fifty or sixty other persons. Six durweeshes, advancing towards him, about two yards, from the semicircle, commenced a zikr; each of them exclaiming, at the same time, '*Allahoo hhai*!' ('God is living!'), and, at each exclamation, beating, with a kind of small and short leather strap, a *baz*, which he held, by a boss at the bottom, in his left hand. This they did for only a few minutes. A black slave then became *melboos*;[6] and rushed into the midst of the durweeshes; throwing his arms about; and exclaiming, 'Allah la la la la la lah!' A person held him, and he soon seemed to recover. The durweeshes, altogether, standing as first described, in the form of a semicircle, then performed a second zikr; each alternate zikkeer exclaiming, '*Allahoo hhai*!' ('God is living!'); and the others, '*Ya hhai*!' (O thou living!'), and all of them bowing at each exclamation, alternately to the right and left. This they continued for about ten minutes. Then, for about the same space of time, in the same manner, and with the same motions, they exclaimed, '*Daim*' ('Everlasting!') and, '*Ya Daim*!' (O Everlasting!').

I felt an irresistible impulse to try if I could do the same without being noticed as an intruder; and accordingly joined the semicircle, and united in the performance; in which I succeeded well enough not to attract observation; but I worked myself into a most uncomfortable heat.—After the zikr just described, a person began to chant a portion of the Ckoor-an: but the zikr was soon resumed; and continued for about a quarter of an hour. Most of the durweeshes there present then kissed the hand of the sheykh; and he retired to an upper apartment.

Such were the exercises whereby the Sufi dervishes sought to reach a sense of exaltation, in which they felt themselves to be in the presence of God. For the great majority, no doubt, these performances were little more than manifestations of animal magnetism, and the sensations they experienced, sometimes assisted by partaking of drugs and stimulants of various kinds,[7] readily to be explained as of the order of hypnosis. But the elect few, who were familiar with the esoteric teachings of their Orders, found the ritual to abound in significant mysteries, and related their successive moods and feelings to the theoretical speculations of the theosophists. In the next chapter we shall describe briefly some of the abstruse ideas which lay at the back of these and similar phenomena.

NINE

THE THEOSOPHY OF ISLAMIC MYSTICISM

THEOSOPHY had seemed a dangerous game to play in Islam since al-Hallāj paid for his indiscreet enthusiasms with his life. Since the preaching of Union with God was liable to misunderstanding and open to the charge of forbidden "incarnationism" (*hulūl*), it was necessary to discover some substitute doctrine which, while coming to much the same port, sailed nearer the wind of orthodoxy. We have seen how al-Hallāj surprisingly took Jesus as his example of a holy man in whom God was incarnate; Sufi theory had only to substitute Muhammad for Jesus, and to moderate the extravagance of al-Hallāj's language, to invent a system of speculative theosophy which would beguile all but the wariest critics. The task was made that much the easier by the existence of an old and honourable tradition of composing panegyrics to God's Messenger in which Muhammad was spoken of in terms of veneration only just short of cult-worship.

It is uncertain who introduced the Logos doctrine into Islam, by which is meant the theory that God's vicegerent controlling the material universe is "the Idea of Muhammad" (*al-haqīqat al-Muhammadīya*); it has been suggested that this doctrine formed a part of al-Ghazālī's esoteric teaching, and that it is hinted at in one of his last works, the *Mishkāt al-anwār*.[1] Likely enough the conception, like many others of later Sufism, had its roots in the secret tradition handed on by word of mouth from the third/ninth century masters. At all events, it successfully resolved the problem of reconciling a transcendent God with a theistic universe. If any man aspired to know God, he might properly seek this end by achieving union with the "Idea of Muhammad," projected by God in pre-eternity to be His likeness—so far as anything may be called God's likeness—and to lead mankind back to Him.

We find this notion fully developed in the writings of Ibn al-Fārid of Cairo (586-632/1181-1235), by far the greatest mystical poet in Arabic literature. His poetry, judged by accepted Western canons, is exceedingly difficult and obscure, and abounds moreover in verbal jugglery which offends our very different taste; its appreciation is rendered all the more hazardous by his fidelity to the conventions of the classical ode of ancient Arabia and his metaphorical use of erotic imagery. Yet, "if his verse abounds in fantastic conceits, if much of it is enigmatic to the last degree, the conceits and enigmas are not, as a rule, rhetorical ornaments or intellectual conjuring tricks, but like tendrils springing from a hidden root are vitally connected with the moods of feeling which they delineate. It may be difficult to believe, what is related on the testimony of his most intimate friends, that he used to dictate his poems at the moment when he came out of a deep ecstatic trance, during which 'he would now stand, now sit, now repose on his side, now lie on his back, wrapped like a dead man; and thus he would pass ten consecutive days, more or less, neither eating nor drinking nor speaking nor stirring.' His style and diction resemble the choicest and finest jewel-work of a fastidious artist rather than the first-fruits of Divine inspiration. Yet I am not inclined to doubt the statement that his poetry was composed in an abnormal manner." [2] So writes the scholar who has done more than anyone else in our time to elucidate Ibn al-Fārid's obscurities and to advance the literary appreciation of his compositions. The following ode, in R.A. Nicholson's translation, illustrates well the poet's use of conventional figures to portray a deep mystical experience. [3]

Where lote-trees o'er the valley cast their shade
The frenzied lover strayed.
Alone with thoughts confusing
Which love put in his brain,
He lost and in his losing
Found the way again:
Lo, on yon gorge's southern slope
The vision long-desired, that seemed far from his hope.
This is 'Aqīq, my friend!
Halt! here to pass were strange.
Feign rapture, if thou be
Not rapt indeed, and let thine eye range free:
Mine, with tears overflowing, cannot range.
Ask the Gazelle that couches in this valley,
Knows he my heart, its passion and distress?
Delighting with his beauty's pride to dally,
He recks not of my love's abasedness.
My dead self be his ransom! 'Tis no giving:
I am all his, dead or living!
Think you he knows that I his absence love
Even as I loved his presence? that I move
Nightly his image to my waking eye?—
A phantasy within a phantasy.
So let me ne'er have savour
Of peace from counsellors, as I never bent
A listening ear towards their argument!
By his sweet grace and favour
I vow my heart tired not, when he did tire,
Of love-desire.
Woe's me, 'Udhayb's fair water might I win
And with its coolness quench the flames within!
But since my longing durst
Not soil that noble stream,
Ah! how I thirst
For its mirage agleam!

While in certain passages Ibn al-Fārid appears to claim no more than union with the Spirit of Muhammad, in others it is difficult to avoid the conclusion that he is pretending to union with God, and in language that lays him open to the charge of pantheism in its extremest form, as in one passage where he writes:[4]

> My degree is of such a height that a man who has not reached it may still be deemed happy; but the state for which I am deemed happy transcends thy degree.
>
> All men are sons of Adam, (and I am as they) save that I alone amongst my brethren have attained to the sobriety of union.
>
> My hearing is like that of Kalīm (Moses) and my heart is informed (about God) by the most excellent (*ahmad*) vision of an eye like that of him who is most excellent (Ahmad = Mohammed).
>
> And my spirit is a spirit to all the spirits (of created beings); and whatsoever thou seest of beauty in the universe flows from the bounty of my nature.
>
> Leave, then, to me (and do not ascribe to anyone else) the knowledge with which I alone was endowed before my appearance (in the phenomenal world), while (after my appearance) amongst created beings my friends knew me not (as I really am).

The Arab commentator on these lines interprets them as implying that Ibn al-Fārid claimed himself to be the Qutb ("Pole" or Logos); but it may be that here and elsewhere he is in fact referring to union with the Idea of Muhammad, and speaking of that Idea as the true Qutb.

Ibn al-Fārid's masterpiece is his great *Tā'iya* (ode rhyming in the letter 't'), a poem of 760 couplets. Judged as an example of rhymer's virtuosity alone, it is an astonishing achievement; when to skill in versifying and amazing dexterity in rhetorical embellishment is added a profundity of thought and a beauty of expression rarely equalled in Arabic literature, it is small wonder that this poem is regarded by Sufis as possessing magical qualities. To conclude this brief sketch of a truly great poet, we give below a translation of the opening lines of the *Tā'iya*, attempting to imitate the rhythm of the original; to mimic the rhymes and verbal play would be impossible in English.

The hand of mine eye gave me of Love's flaming wine to
   take,
Yea, and for cup Her Face, surpassing all loveliness;
Yet did I leave my friends supposing their wine it was
Gladdened my inmost soul, so raptured the glance I gave
(Though of a truth I needed not of my cup to taste,
Having the inward eye, to gaze on Her inward Heart
Amazed), and thereat said thanks to them, my good
   tavern-lads,
That kept me my passion hid, for all my celebrity.
Swiftly I sought Her then—for done were my sober
   days—
No longer by fear held back, but bold in my unrestraint,
Absent the jealous eye, the remnant of self-regard;
And in the privy bridal-chamber I spake with Her
While witnessed my sorry state the flame of the love in me,
Sundered 'twixt self-effacing joy and restoring grief.

If Ibn al-Fārid has had to meet from his orthodox critics
the same kind of charge as that which brought al-Hallāj
to the gallows, the accusation is certainly better founded in
the case of Muhyī al-Dīn Ibn 'Arabī, his famous contemporary, the greatest mystical genius of the Arabs.
Ibn 'Arabī, who traced his lineage from the illustrious
Arabian tribe of Tai, was born at Murcia in 560/1165 and
after studying Traditions and jurisprudence in Seville and
Ceuta moved to Tunis in 590/1194, there to be initiated
into Sufism. Eight years later he journeyed eastwards, and
after residing in Mecca for some time, travelled through
Iraq, Asia Minor and Syria, dying at Damascus in
638/1240. Resembling Swedenborg in more than one
respect, he was like him an exceedingly copious writer;
the Persian poet Jāmī (d.898/1494) says that he composed
more than 500 books [5]; the Egyptian Sufi al-Sha'rānī
(d.973/1565) gives the more conservative estimate of
400 [6]; a modern count of surviving works totals well over
two hundred, [7] and while this list includes many tracts
that run to not more than a dozen pages it also embraces

numerous bulky treatises, among them the massive *al-Futūhāt al-Makkīya*, a veritable Sufi encyclopaedia that has been printed in four large folio volumes. It is upon this work, and its shorter companion the *Fusūs al-hikam*, that Ibn 'Arabī's celebrity chiefly rests; but he was also a poet, after the same formal fashion as Ibn al-Fārid, whom he fully equals in subtlety and obscurity. The following short quotation from the *Tarjumān al-ashwāq*, with a summary of Ibn 'Arabī's own commentary on the verses, is a characteristic example of his style and thought as a poet.[8]

On the day of parting they did not saddle the full-grown reddish-white camels, until they had mounted the peacocks upon them,
Peacocks with murderous glances and sovereign power: thou wouldst fancy that each of them was a Bilqīs on her throne of pearls.
When she walks on the glass pavement thou seest a sun, a celestial sphere in the bosom of Idrīs.
When she kills with her glances, her speech restores to life, as tho' she, in giving life thereby, were Jesus.
Commentary.
" 'The full-grown camels', i.e. the actions inward and outward, for they exalt the good word to Him who is throned on high, as He hath said: '*And the good deed exalts it*' (Kor. xxxv, 11). 'The peacocks' mounted on them are his loved ones: he likens them to peacocks because of their beauty. The peacocks are the spirits of those actions, for no action is acceptable or good or fair until it hath a spirit consisting in the intention or desire of its doer.
'With murderous glances and sovereign power': he refers to the Divine wisdom which accrues to a man in his hours of solitude, and which assaults him with such violence that he is unable to behold his personality.
'A Bilqīs on her throne of pearls': he refers to that which was manifested to Gabriel and to the Prophet during his night journey upon the bed of pearl and jacinth in the terrestrial heaven. The author calls the Divine wisdom 'Bilqīs' on account of its being the child of theory, which is subtle, and practice, which is gross, just

as Bilqīs was both spirit and woman, since her father was
of the Jinn and her mother was of mankind.

The mention of Idrīs alludes to her lofty and exalted
rank. 'In the bosom of Idrīs,' i.e. under his control, in
respect of his turning her wheresoever he will, as the
Prophet said: 'Do not bestow wisdom on those who are
unworthy of it, lest ye do it a wrong.' The opposite case is
that of one who speaks because he is dominated by his
feeling (hāl), and who is therefore under the control of an
influence (wārid). In this verse the author calls attention
to his puissance in virtue of a prophetic heritage, for the
prophets are masters of their spiritual feelings (ahwāl),
whereas most of the saints are mastered by them.

'She kills with her glances': referring to the station of
passing-away in contemplation (al-fanā fi 'l-mushāhada).
'Her speech restores to life': referring to the completion of the
moulding of man when the spirit was breathed into him.

The foregoing quotation is thoroughly typical of Ibn
'Arabī's extraordinary complexity, not to say confusion, of
mental outlook, which renders his writings so very baffling
to the student, and so intractable to the translator. He
gathered into the comprehensive range of his meditation
the entire learning of Islam, and was perfectly familiar
not only with the writings and teachings of the orthodox
Sunni theologians, lawyers and philosophers, and of the
Sufis from the earliest times to his own day, but also with
the schismatic and heretical movements like the Mu'-
tazilites, Carmathians and Isma'ilis. His system, vast and
widely ranging as it is, embraces the speculations and
terminologies of all his widely various sources; so that the
problem of abstruse reference is complicated by the further
constant difficulty of an inconsistent technical vocabulary.
It is obviously impossible in a few paragraphs even to hint
at more than a minute fraction of his multifarious
teachings, but the following notes will indicate how he
ties up with some of his predecessors and influences his
successors. [9]

(1) God is Absolute Being, and is the sole source of all existence; in Him alone Being and Existence are one and inseparable.

(2) The Universe possesses Relative Being, either actual or potential; it is both eternal-existent and temporal-non-existent; eternal-existent as being in God's knowledge, and temporal-non-existent as being external to God.

(3) God is both Transcendent and Immanent, transcendence and immanence being two fundamental aspects of Reality as man knows it. "The *Haqq* (Reality) of whom transcendence is asserted is the same as the *Khalq* (Creation) of whom immanence is asserted although (logically) the creator is distinguished from the created."[10]

(4) Being, apart from God, exists by virtue of God's Will, acting in accordance with the laws proper to the things thus existent; His agents are the Divine Names, or universal concepts.

(5) Before coming into existence, things of the phenomenal world were latent in the Mind of God as fixed prototypes (*a'yān thābita*), and were thus one with the Divine Essence and Consciousness; these prototypes are intermediaries between the One as Absolute Reality and the Phenomenal World.

(6) There is no such thing as Union with God in the sense of becoming one with God, but there is the realisation of the already existing fact that the mystic *is* one with God.

(7) The creative, animating and rational principle of the Universe, or the First Intellect, is the Reality (Idea) of Muhammad (*al-Haqīqat al-Muhammadīya*), also called the Reality of Realities (*Haqīqat al-haqā'iq*); this principle finds its fullest manifestation in the Perfect Man (*al-Insān al-kāmil*).

(8) Each prophet is *a* Logos of God; *the* Logos is Muhammad, the "head" of the hierarchy of prophets. All

these individual logoi are united in the Reality of Muhammad.

(9) The Perfect Man is a miniature of Reality; he is the microcosm, in whom are reflected all the perfect attributes of the macrocosm. Just as the Reality of Muhammad was the *creative principle* of the Universe, so the Perfect Man was the *cause* of the Universe, being the epiphany of God's desire to be known; for only the Perfect Man knows God, loves God, and is loved by God. For Man alone the world was made.

Ibn 'Arabī has a special doctrine of Saintship (*wilāya*). He takes the view that all prophets are also saints, but that the saintly aspect of each prophet is higher than the prophetic aspect. All prophets and saints are manifestations of the Spirit or Reality of Muhammad; and the historical Muhammad is superior to all other prophets by virtue of his office as Seal of the Prophets (*Khātim al-anbiyā'*). However he hints, and in fact explicitly declares, that there is also a Seal of the Saints (*Khātim al-auliyā'*) who is the *perfect* manifestation of the Spirit of Muhammad; he states that this Seal "is born in our time: I have met him and seen the mark of the Seal which he had on him"[11]; he further claims, "I am the Seal of the saintship, no doubt, (the Seal of) the heritage of the Hashimite (Muhammad) and the Messiah"[12]; from this and other passages in his writings it seems fair to deduce that he did in fact regard himself as the Seal of the Saints.

Ibn 'Arabī marks a turning-point in the history of speculative Sufism. Though he was violently attacked for his pantheistic teachings (yet his system can be regarded as monistic rather than pantheistic) and for his extravagant claims, no mystic who came after him was free of his influence, and he has left his mark on all subsequent mystical literature. This is not the place to discuss his impact on mediaeval Christian mysticism, and it is sufficient to remark that the matter is now commonly accepted as proven. To indicate in a small way the nature of the perpetuation of his ideas in later Islamic writings, it will be enough to recall that the Persian poet 'Irāqī (d.688/1289) composed his *Lama'āt* after hearing Sadr al-Dīn Qonawī (d. 672/1273) lecture on Ibn 'Arabī's *Fusūs al-hikam*, and that Jāmī not only compiled a commentary on the *Lama'āt* but also composed his *Lawā'ih* in emulation of that work. These two artistic little treatises, which are in line of descent from the Persian book *Sawānih* by al-Ghazālī's brother Ahmad (d.517/1123), have as their special theme the doctrine of the mystical trinity of Love, Lover and Beloved, which they interpret along the lines of Ibn 'Arabī's theosophy. The following is a rendering of the introductory section of the *Lama'āt*.

Praise be to God, Who hath lit up the countenance of His beloved with Beauty's revelations   so that he gleamed with light   and saw therein Perfection's manifestations   and joyed in him with true delight—
Who set him up before Him, choosing him, while Adam was yet a thing unremembered quite   while never Tablet was inscribed and Pen did nothing write—
   storehouse he of all that is   key of Bounty's treasuries   Zion of every heart's desire   Lord of the banner of praise and of that rank whereunto all souls do aspire   whose most exalted tongue doth say: Though Adam's son in outward form I seem,   My fatherhood is proved by inward gleam.

'Though Form,' he said, 'proclaims me Adam's son,
My true degree a higher place hath won.
When in the glass of Beauty I behold,
The Universe my image doth enfold:
In Heaven's Sun behold me manifest—
Each tiny molecule doth me attest.
My Essence true all holy Spirits prove,
And in my Shape all human Forms do move.
Ocean's a drop from my pervading Sea,

Light but a flash of my vast Brilliancy:
From Throne to Carpet, all that is doth seem
Naught but a Mote that rides the sunlit Beam.
When Being's Veil of Attributes is shed,
My Splendour o'er a lustrous World is spread.
That water which to Khizr gave life unending
Behold! from Kausar's heavenly Fount descending:
That breath of Christ which quickened Life from Death
The afflatus is of my Soul-nurturing Breath.
In all that is, I manifest, in fine:
Yea, and the Greatest Name of God is mine!'

God bless him, and grant him abundant peace!
To proceed: a few words in exposition of the ranks of
Love, after the fashion of the *Sawānih*, dictated by the
tongue of the moment, that every lover may have a
mirror displaying the Beloved; though in truth Love has
too high a rank, that any by virtue of understanding or
exposition should approach the curtain of its Majesty,
to gaze with the eye of revelation and the open vision
upon the Beauty of its Reality.

Love soars beyond the Reach of Human Mind,
By Parting and Reunion unconfined:
    Whene'er a thing o'er Fancy rides supreme,
Image is vain, and Comprehension blind.

It is hidden by the Veil of Glory, and dwells alone in the
self-sufficiency of Perfection: the veils of its Essence are
its Qualities, which are themselves comprehended in that
Essence. Its Majesty is the lover of its Beauty, and its
Beauty is comprehended by its Majesty. For ever it makes
love to itself, and with naught else concerns itself: every
instant it raises the veil from the face of Belovedness,
and each moment lifts up a new song of its Loverhood.

Love sings a song within the Veil:
Ho, lover! listen to his tale.
New airs each moment he doth raise,
Each instant lifts new songs of praise.
The whole World echoes with his song:
Was ever Voice so sweet and strong?

The Universe his secret knows:
Could Echo keep his secret close?
This mystery each Atom tells:
No need have I to utter spells.

Every instant, with every tongue, Love whispers its own
secret into its own ear; every moment, with every ear, it
hears its own words uttered by its own tongue. Every
minute, with every eye, it reveals its own beauty to its
own regard; every second, in every aspect, it presents
its own being to itself as witness.

In silence and in speech He talks with me,
In flashing eye, and eyelid's modesty.

Knowest thou what story Love whispers in my ears?

'I am Love: in all the world I have no home.
I am Anqa of the West: unseen I roam.
Earth and Heaven have I ta'en, with Eye and Brow:
Neither bow nor shaft have I, yet ask not how;
Like the Sun in every Atom I am shewn,
Yet in Light's Transcendency abide unknown.
Every Tongue my Word bears, with all Ears I hear:
Mystery how strange, I have not Tongue nor Ear!
Since that every Living Thing I am Alone,
Unto me in Earth and Heaven like is none'.

To round off this brief panorama of the later meta-
physics of Sufism, let us glance at the doctrine of the
Perfect Man as developed by 'Abd al-Karīm al-Jīlī
(d.832/1428) in his famous book *al-Insān al-kāmil*.
Accepting Ibn 'Arabī's conception of the Unity of Being
(*wahdat al-wujūd*), he traces the descent of Pure Being,
which in itself is without name and attribute, through
three successive stages of manifestation which he calls
Oneness (*ahadīya*), He-ness (*huwīya*), and I-ness (*anīya*).
" Man, in virtue of his essence, is the cosmic Thought
assuming flesh and connecting Absolute Being with the
world of Nature."[13] Through three corresponding stages

of mystical illumination (*tajallī*), the mystic may aspire to retrace the order of his descent and finally, by becoming the Perfect Man, being stripped of every attribute, return once more as Absolute to the Absolute. The idea of the descent of the Universal Spirit into matter, and of the purgative ascent of man out of matter, was of course familiar to Sufi thought long before al-Jīlī's time; his particular merit is that of crystallising the conception, under the influence of Ibn 'Arabī's general system, into a clear and consistent metaphysic. To see how long are the shadows cast by these great figures of mediaeval Islamic mysticism, we may notice that the late Sir Muhammad Iqbal (d.1938), who had made a detailed study of Sufi thought, appears to have derived his special theory of Higher Selfhood in part out of the Sufi doctrine of the Perfect Man and in part from the Superman of German philosophy culminating in Nietzsche.

TEN

THE PERSIAN POETS

FROM the foregoing review of Sufism in Arabic literature it will have been observed that the Arabs, or non-Arabs writing in Arabic, stressed in particular the philosophical side of Islamic mysticism, and devoted especial care to constructing a stable theosophical system. If Sufism had given birth to nothing more than a lofty ethic and a subtle metaphysic, it might have been allowed that the movement had made a substantial contribution to human thought and experience. But when Sufism gripped the mind and soul of Iran, and the abounding poetic imagination of the Persians discovered this new theatre to display itself, Islamic mysticism developed aesthetically in a manner soaring high above the ranges of pure speculation. Classical Persian poetry is to a very notable extent Sufi in content and inspiration.

The Sufi poetry of Persia (and what is said of Persian poetry here applies equally to Turkish and Urdu) falls into three main categories, and will be reviewed under these heads—didactic, romantic and lyrical. The first Persian author to write an extensive poem elaborating the doctrines of Sufism was Sanā'ī, whose literary activities cover the first half of the 6/12th century. He was a prolific poet, composing very freely in the two classical forms of Qasīda (ode) and Ghazal (lyric), as well as in Rubā'īyāt (quatrains) and Mathnawī (rhyming couplets) ; it was in the fourth of these forms that he wrote his epic *Hadīqat al-haqīqa*, which set up a model followed by later authors. This work may perhaps best be regarded as an attempt to put into verse what Arab writers like al-Sarrāj, al-Qushairī and al-Ansārī had put into prose; it is a general survey of ascetic, ethical and mystical thought, illustrated and enlivened by anecdotes of saints and mystics. Rūmī, a far greater thinker and poet, freely acknowledged his indebtedness to Sanā'ī, not only quoting from the *Hadīqa* in his own *Mathnawī*, but also in direct confession :—

> Attar was the spirit,
>   Sanai his eyes twain,
> And in time thereafter
>   Came we in their train.

Farīd al-Dīn 'Attār, who flourished some sixty years after Sanā'ī, was an even more productive author; not only did he compose easily in all the categories of verse, but he also wrote a valuable and highly esteemed treatise on the biographies of Muslim saints and mystics (*Tadhkirat al-auliyā'*). His numerous *mathnawī* poems include three of first rate importance, the *Asrār-nāma* ('Book of Secrets') on general Sufi principles, the *Ilāhī-nāma* ('Divine Book') on mystical love, and the *Mantiq al-tair* ('Speech of Birds'), a splendid allegory portraying the mystic's progress towards Union with God. The first two of these works have not been translated, but the third is available to English readers in an abridged version by Edward FitzGerald. [1]

> Once on a time from all the Circles seven
> Between the stedfast Earth and rolling Heaven
> The Birds, of all Note, Plumage, and Degree,
> That float in Air, and roost upon the Tree;
> And they that from the Waters snatch their Meat,
> And they that scour the Desert with long Feet:
> Birds of all Natures, known or not to Man,
> Flock'd from all Quarters into full Divan,
> On no less solemn business than to find,
> Or choose, a Sultan Khalif of their kind,
> For whom, if never theirs, or lost, they pined.

So begins FitzGerald's epitome. The conclusion of the
story shews the Birds reaching their goal, and in doing so,
realising the truth of the Sufi mystery of self-effacement in
Divine Union.

> Then cried the Spokesman, 'Be it even so:
> Let us but see the Fount from which we flow,
> And, seeing, lose Ourselves therein!' And, Lo!
> Before the Word was utter'd, or the Tongue
> Of Fire replied, or Portal open flung,
> They were *within*—they were before the *Throne*,
> Before the Majesty that sat thereon,
> But wrapt in so insufferable a Blaze
> Of Glory as beat down their baffled Gaze,
> Which, downward dropping, fell upon a Scroll
> That, Lightning-like, flash'd back on each the whole
> Past half-forgotten Story of his Soul:
> Like that which Yūsuf in his Glory gave
> His brethren as some Writing he would have
> Interpreted; and at a Glance, behold
> Their own Indenture for their Brother sold!
> And so with these poor Thirty: who, abasht
> In Memory all laid bare and Conscience lasht,
> By full Confession and Self-loathing flung
> The Rags of carnal Self that round them clung;
> And, their old selves self-knowledged and self-loathed,
> And in the Soul's Integrity re-clothed,
> Once more they ventured from the Dust to raise
> Their Eyes—up to the Throne—into the Blaze,
> And in the Centre of the Glory there
> Beheld the Figure of—*Themselves*—as 't were
> Transfigured—looking to Themselves, beheld
> The Figure on the Throne en-miracled,
> Until their Eyes themselves and *That* between
> Did hesitate which *Sëer* was, which *Seen*;
> They That, That They: Another, yet the Same;
> Dividual, yet One: from whom there came
> A Voice of awful Answer, scarce discern'd
> From *which* to Aspiration *whose* return'd
> They scarcely knew; as when some Man apart
> Answers aloud the Question in his Heart—

The Sun of my Perfection is a Glass
Wherein from *Seeing* into *Being* pass
All who, reflecting as reflected see
Themselves in Me, and Me in Them; not *Me*,
But all of Me that a contracted Eye
Is comprehensive of Infinity:
Nor yet *Themselves*; no Selves, but of The All
Fractions, from which they split and whither fall.
As Water lifted from the Deep, again
Falls back in individual Drops of Rain
Then melts into the Universal Main.
All you have been, and seen, and done, and thought,
Not *You* but *I*, have seen and been and wrought:
I was the Sin that from Myself rebell'd:
I the Remorse that tow'rd Myself compelled:
I was the Tajidar who led the Track:
I was the litle Briar that pull'd you back:
Sin and Contrition—Retribution owed,
And cancell'd—Pilgrim, Pilgrimage, and Road,
Was but Myself toward Myself: and Your
Arrival but *Myself* at my own Door:
Who in your Fraction of Myself behold
Myself within the Mirror Myself hold
To see Myself in, and each part of Me
That sees himself, though drown'd, shall ever see.
Come you lost Atoms to your Centre draw,
And *be* the Eternal Mirror that you saw:
Rays that have wander'd into Darkness wide
Return, and back into your Sun subside.

Nizāmī, of the same brilliant period of Persian poetry, who is otherwise famous as the supreme exponent of the romantic idyll, composed as the first of his five narrative poems (*Khamsa*) a treatise somewhat after the fashion of Sanā'ī's *Hadīqa*, entitled *Makhzan al-asrār* ('Treasury of Secrets'). However, he was not a true mystic of the calibre of Sanā'ī and 'Attār, but rather an encomiast of piety and poverty; when he found that this style of composition brought no substantial reward, he turned his hand successfully to more mundane themes. He wrote with

great learning and brilliancy, and his Hymns to the
Deity are notably fine.

> *In Allah's Name, the Kind, the Pitying*:
> This Key unlocks the Treasury of the King.
> With God all Thoughts arise, all Words descend;
> Then let His Name thy Recitation end.
> Before the Birth of Beings transient,
> Ere every Essence lasting, permanent,
> This timeless World accepts His Regimen,
> His Fingers grace the Everlasting Pen.
> His Hand unveils the Mysteries of the Skies,
> Yet veils the Secrets of the truly Wise.
> Sole Origin of goodly Essences,
> Sole Source of every Thing that living is,
> He dights the Sun with glowing Jewelry,
> He clothes with grass the Earth, with gems the Sea.
> All leaders of the Faith by Him are led,
> He giveth Bread to All who live by Bread.
> He threads with Pearls the single-corded Mind,
> He lights the Intellect that else were blind:
> He marks their Brow who live in Piety,
> And to the sceptred King gives Sovranty.
> He brings to naught what heedless Men design,
> But spares their Sins who unto Him repine:
> He stills the Clamour of the fearful Heart,
> And, to the Knowing, Counsel doth impart.
> First He and Last, in All that is and lives,
> Naughts Being, and to Nothing Being gives:
> Before His Might the two Worlds sink to death,
> The Sum of all our days is but a Breath . . .
> Nizami's Clay, that by His Feet is trod,
> A Furrow is, where grows the Seed of God. [2]

The unsurpassable summit in this form of composition
was reached by the illustrious Jalāl al-Dīn Rūmī
(d.672/1273), a native of Balkh who migrated with his
father to Konia in Asia Minor and there, as we have seen,
became the eponymous founder of the Mevlevi Order of
dervishes. As Ibn 'Arabī summed up and gathered into a

single system all that had been said on mysticism in Arabic before him, so Rumi in his immortal *Mathnawī* performed a like service in Persian. This vast poem, which has been fully translated and commented in English, [3] ranges over the entire field of Sufi speculation; the anecdotes that intersperse the discourse are brilliantly told, abounding in wisdom and humour. A previous volume in this series by the late Professor R. A. Nicholson deals so adequately with Rūmī's life, thought and style that it is scarcely necessary to go into further detail here, and we may content ourselves by quoting his version of the opening lines of the *Mathnawī* in which Rūmī, as so often, uses the imagery of the reed-pipe to portray the mystic's desolate cry to God.

> Hearken to this Reed forlorn,
> Breathing, ever since 'twas torn
> From its rushy bed, a strain
> Of impassioned love and pain.
>
> The secret of my song, though near,
> None can see and none can hear.
> Oh, for a friend to know the sign
> And mingle all his soul with mine!
>
> 'Tis the flame of Love that fired me,
> 'Tis the wine of Love inspired me.
> Wouldst thou learn how lovers bleed,
> Hearken, hearken to the Reed!

The marriage of romance to mysticism took place early in the history of the Sufi movement; as we have seen, the language of human love was used freely to describe the relations between the mystic and his Divine Beloved. The Persian love of allegory, which we have remarked in the prose writings of Suhrawardī Maqtūl, rendered this new convention all the more popular and pleasing. One of the favourite themes was the story of Joseph and Potiphar's wife as recounted in the Koran; the best known of many poems on this subject is the *Yūsuf Zulaikhā* of Jāmī (d.898/1492).[4] The same prolific writer, whose name has already occurred several times in these pages, spiritualised other familiar love-stories, such as the desert tragedy of Lailā and her mad lover-poet (*Majnūn Lailā*),[5] and the tale of Salāmān and Absāl which Hunain b. Ishāq the translator of Plato and Aristotle first introduced into Arabic, and FitzGerald summarised in English verse. We may take as a sort of mystical romance the remarkable Pilgrim's Progress (*Sair al-'ibād*) of Sanā'ī, which has been compared with Dante's *Divina Commedia*, though on a miniature scale[6]; the descriptions of personified vices are uncommonly powerful.

> When from this evil folk we took the road,
> We came unto another wild abode;
> A devils' paradise my gaze befell,
> A people smothered by the smoke of hell.
> Savage they were, and black as thundercloud
> Shrouding a mountaintop, that steely crowd
> All hushed and silent, as if unaware
> Bewildered at each other they would stare,
> All full of wind and air, as bagpipes be,
> Eke with two necks and orifices three;
> Monkeys they were, all running at a bound,
> Head chasing tail, as will a fox a hound,
> Wind-full and crooked, like a lute or reed,
> Yellow, and cold, and ponderous as lead.
> Their heads, as irises, were all an eye,
> Bodies like plane-trees stretching hands on high;
> And thus the twain, one upward, one below,
> Pushed out both paws to work the people woe;
> With temper dull, and penetrating sight,
> Faces lack-lustre, eyes as black as night,
> Eyes that were founts of modest plenitude,
> Faces that ravenously searched for food.

It was above all in lyric that Persian mysticism found its highest expression, and there are few poets who have not contributed something to this form. The Ghazal was originally a short love-poem—the Arabic word signifies "the talk of youths and maidens"—and had had a distinguished career in Arabic literature before the Persians took it over for the same purpose. Sanā'ī was the first to compose abundantly in this form with religious intention, and if he did not actually invent the allegory of the mystical lyric he certainly took it far upon its path of evolution. But before touching at greater length upon the progress of the Persian Ghazal, it will be convenient to offer some remarks on the imagery used by the mystical poets in this type of composition, as otherwise its allusions, which alone give it religious value, are entirely wasted upon the reader who has to depend upon translations. The table which follows is based upon a curious little pamphlet entitled *Risāla-yi Mishwāq*, by Muhsin Faid Kāshānī, a Persian Sufi author of the 11/17th century who was concerned to defend the mystical poets against their orthodox critics, and to clear them of charges based on too literal an interpretation of their technical vocabulary.

Rukh (face, cheek): the revelation of Divine Beauty in Attributes of Grace, e.g. the Gracious, the Clement, the Life-giving, the Guide, the Bountiful; Light; Divine Reality.

Zulf (tress): the revelation of Divine Majesty in Attributes of Omnipotence, e.g. the Withholder, the Seizer, the Omnipotent, the Death-giver, the Deluder; Darkness; phenomena as a veil concealing Divine Reality.

Khāl (mole): the point of Real Unity, which is concealed and is therefore represented as black.

Khatt (down on the cheek): the manifestation of Reality in spiritual forms.

Chashm (eye): God's beholding His servants and their

aptitudes. The "eye" is said to be *mast* (intoxicated) or *bīmār* (languishing) to indicate that God has no need of man, and pays no heed to him. The *ghamza* (glance) of the "eye" refers to God's granting of spiritual repose after anguish, or anguish after repose.

Abrū (eyebrow): God's Attributes, which veil His Essence.

Lab (lip): the life-giving property of God, and His keeping man in existence. The *dahān* (mouth) is said to be *tang* (narrow) as a reference to the fact that the source of man's being is invisible.

Sharāb (wine): ecstatic experience due to the revelation of the True Beloved, destroying the foundations of reason.

Sāqī (wine-bearer): Reality, as loving to manifest itself in every form that is revealed.

Jām (cup): the revelations of (Divine) Acts.

Sabū (pitcher), *Khum* (jar): the revelations of (Divine) Names and Qualities.

Bahr (sea), *Qulzum* (ocean): the revelations of the (Divine) Essence. The whole seen and unseen world is like a *khumkhāna* (vault) containing the wine of Being and the inborn love of God; each atom of the world, according to its receptivity and particular aptitude, is a *paimāna* (goblet) of the wine of His love, and the goblet is full of this wine.

Kharābāt (tavern): Pure Unity (*wahdat*), undifferentiated and unqualified.

Kharābātī (tavern-haunter): the true lover who is freed from the chains of discrimination, knowing that all acts, and the qualities of all things, are obliterated in the Divine Acts and Qualities.

But (idol): every object of worship other than God. Sometimes it is used to indicate a manifestation of the Divine Beauty, to worship which is the same as worshipping its Creator; sometimes it connotes a Perfect Man (*kāmil*) or a Guide (*murshid*) who is the Pole (*quṭb*) of his time. The *zunnār* (girdle) is a symbol for taking the compact of obedience and service.

Kufr-i haqīqī (true infidelity): concealing the existence of multiplicity and differentiation in the Being of God; this "gnostics' infidelity" is the same as true Islam and faith.

Tarsā'ī (godfearing, Christianity): deliverance from the bondage of (hypocritical) traditional belief (*taqlīd*), quitting the chains of custom and habit. *Tarsā-bachcha* (Christian child) denotes the perfect guide.

It is against the background of this allegory of love and worship, of faithlessness and shame, that the lyrics of Sanā'ī, 'Attar, Rūmī, 'Irāqi, Maghribī, Amīr Khusrau, Sa'dī, Hāfiz, Jāmī and many another must be read; I have attempted in my *Immortal Rose* to give a few illustrations of the development of this school of poetry, and would refer the reader curious for examples to that anthology. But the matter is not altogether free of difficulties and complexities, for several of the Sufi poets were at the same time earning their livelihood by courting kings and princes, and many of their lyrics must be regarded as double allegories—the reference is made simultaneously to the Divine Beloved, and to the very earthly patron whose favour is no less difficult to win. This caution seems to be especially necessary in the case of Hāfiz, but Sanā'ī and Sa'dī are also to be handled with care. Running through all the poets—and even Rūmī comes into this— there is also an element of human affection, so that the visible object of regard, be he a handsome young Sufi or a revered preceptor, shares with God the poet's passionate addresses.

The allegory of wine raises its own separate problems. There are those who take every reference to the crimson cup as intending spiritual intoxication, and even 'Umar

Khaiyām has sometimes been interpreted after this fashion. But it is a difficult position to maintain consistently; while one can be confident that such austere mystics as 'Attār, Rūmī and Jāmī were wholly innocent in their use of this dangerous imagery, it is by no means to be imagined that others employing the language of the tavern did not refer to a literal as well as a metaphorical drunkenness. There is also a third kind of intoxication, the intoxication of the intellect, what I have referred to elsewhere as the philosophy of unreason[7]; I believe this to be the implication of Hāfiz' wine-vocabulary, and most likely too of 'Umar Khaiyām's.

While the language of love and wine is common to all the Persian mystical poets, Rūmī stands out supreme in this convention and technique too, not indeed for stylistic perfection—Sa'dī and Hāfiz are his superiors there—but for inventiveness of imagery and fertility of allusion. He superimposes upon the general foundation of Sufi metaphor several new ranges of comparison; one category he derives from the ritual of his religious Order, with its dancing and music, so that the drum, the reed-pipe, the whirling movements of the dervishes, all have their special mystic meanings. Rūmī is particularly fascinated by the idea of rotation, and under the inspiration of the Mevlevi dance he invents a wonderful symbolism of circling spheres and planets, of mill-wheel and mill-stone.

> Thy mountain of the sun
> I'll fashion to a mill,
> And as my waters run.
> I'll turn thee at my will.

All natural phenomena come within the gamut of his imagery; at time he seems to identify his mystical moods with the changing face of nature about him.

Men have argued (but they lied)
That this image does not bide;
One declared we are a tree,
Said another, grass are we.

Yet the rustling of this bough
Proves the breeze is stirring now;
Silent then, O silent be:
That we are, and this are we.

Not only in his lyrics, but also and perhaps still more in
his quatrains, Rūmī draws images of surprising beauty
out of his own spiritual consciousness, establishing an
irrefutable claim to be the greatest mystical poet Islam,
and perhaps the world, has ever produced.

I sought a soul in the sea,
And found a coral there;
Beneath the foam for me
An ocean was all laid bare.

Into my heart's night
Along a narrow way
I groped; and lo! the light,
An infinite land of day.

What other poet in so few words and with such exquisite
imagery has ever told the whole story of the soul's quest
for God? Or in another quatrain:—

Happy was I
In the pearl's heart to lie;
Till, lashed by life's hurricane,
Like a tossed wave I ran.

The secret of the sea
I uttered thunderously;
Like a spent cloud on the shore
I slept, and stirred no more."

Here is epitomised the entire history of the phenomenal world, as viewed by the mystic—the progress of man out of God, into the universe, and back again to God. And there we will leave this very brief and very inadequate review of Persian mystical poetry, the supreme artistic expression of mysticism in Islam, with an invitation to those interested to look further at the not inconsiderable volume of translations that many English hands have made. [8]

ELEVEN

THE DECAY OF SUFISM

THE age of Ibn al-Fāriḍ, Ibn 'Arabī and Rūmī represents the climax of Sufi achievement, both theoretically and artistically. Thereafter, although through the numerous and ever multiplying Religious Orders the influence of Sufi thought and practice became constantly more widespread, and though sultans and princes did not disdain to lend the movement their patronage and personal adherence—a striking example is the noble and pathetic figure of Dārā Shikoh, son of the Mogul emperor Shāh Jahān, who wrote a number of books on Sufism, in one of which, the *Majma' al-bahrain*,[1] he sought to reconcile its theory with the Vedanta—the signs of decay appear more and more clearly, and abuse and scandal assail and threaten to destroy its fair reputation.

It was inevitable, as soon as legends of miracles became attached to the names of the great mystics, that the credulous masses should applaud imposture more than true devotion; the cult of saints, against which orthodox Islam ineffectually protested, promoted ignorance and superstition, and confounded charlatanry with lofty speculation. To live scandalously, to act impudently, to speak unintelligibly—this was the easy highroad to fame, wealth and power.

The history of the decline varies from country to country according to circumstance, but the general pattern, though admitting differences of detail, is fairly consistent throughout. In the present sketch, the situation as it developed in Egypt will be taken as a typical example:

at the same time it must be remarked that the study of this period of degeneration is still in its initial stages.

A modern Egyptian researcher has dated the decline of true Sufism in his country from the political and economic disorders of the second half of the 9/15th and the beginning of the 10/16th centuries. [2] Though this is perhaps too broad a generalisation—for there can be little doubt that the decay set in considerably earlier—it is certainly true that Sufism shared in the general collapse of learning which preceded the Ottoman conquest. The picture drawn of Sufi life in those times reveals how completely unreason had triumphed over the sober speculation and steadfast piety of the great mystics. Not only did the popular "saints" exhibit the utmost contempt for the ritual obligations of Islam, so that they made a boast of not performing the prayers—and one, Barakāt al-Khaiyāt (d.923/1517), on being pressed by the Mufti and Ulema of the Azhar to accompany them to Friday prayer, obliged them by performing the ritual ablutions in filthy water—but they also treated the secular rulers of the country with outrageous impertinence. As for the example they offered to the public at large, the story is told how ʿAlī Wahīsh (d.917/1511) made a special point of displaying his bestialism on the common highway whenever opportunity presented itself. [3]

The neglect of religious ordinance and moral order was serious enough; even more disastrous was the contempt for all learning, which now masqueraded in the threadbare garb of piety. For whatever the Sufis of old may have been—and many of them were openly hostile to orthodoxy and bold against authority of every kind—they generally maintained a decent respect for study, and constantly had upon their lips the Prophet's injunction to "seek learning, even if it be from China." The new Sufis, however, made boast of ignorance, which they were indeed interested to applaud in the masses, for it secured them from rational attack and lent credence to their claims of miraculous powers. Meanwhile magic assumed an increasing importance in their repertory. Early Sufism had been refreshingly free of this most mischievous variety of mystification and obscurantism; in this age of decline, as in all similar times, charms and amulets came to acquire a special value in the eyes of men no longer confident against the vicissitudes of fortune; cabbalism and witchcraft provided an attractive substitute for defeated reason.

The Religious Orders spread their influence and their organisation throughout the country, ruling the masses through a well-planned hierarchy that allowed the freest regional autonomy. Every village or group of villages acquired its local saint, to be supported and revered during his lifetime, worshipped and capitalised after his death. Few indeed were the voices that dared protest against this ruinous order of things, for politician and theologian alike feared to oppose the true masters, and found it easier and more profitable to share in the swindle. One brave spirit of the eighteenth century, al-Badr al-Hijāzī, denounced the prevailing abuses in verses that are as vigorous as they are ungrammatical.[4]

> Would that we had not lived to see every demented madman held up by his fellows as a 'Pole'!
> Their ulema take refuge in him; indeed, they have even adopted him as a Lord, instead of the Lord of the Throne;
> For they have forgotten God, saying, 'So-and-so provides deliverance from suffering for all mankind.'
> When he dies, they make him the object of pilgrimage, and hasten to his shrine, Arabs and foreigners alike:
> Some kiss his grave, and some the threshold of his door, and the dust—

> So do the infidels behave towards their idols, seeking
> thereby to win their favour.
> And that is due to blindness of vision: woe to the man
> whose heart God has blinded!

Such was the dark side of Sufism in its last phase. It is a
picture familiar enough from the accounts of travellers
in the Muslim world during the eighteenth and nineteenth
centuries; and it is the picture that is all too present before
the eyes of modern Muslim thinkers when they write on
Sufism in general. It is understandable that the renaissance
of learning in Islam should have been accompanied by a
violent reaction against the abuses and superstitions which
were rightly regarded as important causes of the back-
wardness of these peoples. Sufism was now increasingly
the prime target of attack for those wrathful intellectuals
who desired to see their countries independent, and their
countrymen delivered from the bondage of spiritual
enslavement. Though the Sufi Orders continued—and in
many countries continue—to hold the interest and
allegiance of the ignorant masses, no man of education
would care to speak in their favour.

Yet while admitting the deplorable effects of superstition allied to mystification, it would surely be unjust to
pretend that Sufism, even in the last stages of its decay,
did not retain some noble and ennobling elements, or
that its influence at its most degraded period was wholly
evil. Though no doubt the majority of these professional
mystics were either hypocrites or self-deluded, and
battened on the credulity of their followers, the movement
never at any time lacked for a few sincere men of high
principles and true faith, whose example shed a brave
light in the surrounding darkness of ignorance and misery.
It is in any case debatable whether, in circumstances of
catastrophic wretchedness, it is better to preach dissatis-
faction, after the modern fashion of unscrupulous agitators,

or to advocate resignation, as the Sufis did. The political intriguer is ready to guarantee an earthly paradise as the swift reward for murderous insurrection; but those peoples among whom murder and insurrection have had free play do not appear to have approached very appreciably towards the promised land. The mystic holds out the prospect of present tranquillity and future bliss as the consequence of accepting God's Will; the first part of their programme is certainly fulfilled, so that men who lack not courage and resource are able to suffer the most shocking blows of fortune without losing their faith and human dignity. It is easy to laugh at the follies of credulity; but is not credulity itself but the poor relation of faith? And without faith, hope withers and love dies, and all the light goes out of life.

Even in its death-throes Sufism gave birth to a man of no small genius, whose life and writings mirror faithfully the worst as well as the best of this final period. 'Abd al-Wahhāb al-Sha'rānī (898-973/1493-1565) lived through the ruin of Mamluk rule and the subjugation of Egypt to the Turks, yet he was learned in all the Muslim sciences, and himself wrote upwards of sixty books, mostly Sufi in character. A Western critic has appraised him as "a comprehensive and honest scholar of wide education but uncritical and highly superstitious. His tremendous exaggeration of his own value is an unpleasant feature in him; he usually boasts of his own works that they were pioneers and nothing similar existed on the particular subject. But the honesty, uprightness and enthusiasm of his character, his championship of justice, humanity and toleration, his sincerity and the frankness with which he holds up the modesty of the Christians and Jews as a pattern for the 'Ulamā, and finally his high respect for the dignity of womanhood all make an exceedingly favourable impression." [5]

In point of fact there is nothing very original about al-Sha'rānī's doctrines; he is content, like all in this period of decline, to epitomise and annotate the writings of the great masters, shaping the pattern alike of his life and his thought to the model they invented so long ago. One of his most interesting and voluminous works is a sort of autobiography, the *Latā'if al-minan*, in which he renders thanks to God in detail for manifold blessings received over a long life of piety and devotion. Here, as elsewhere in his writings, he is not in the least inclined to be modest about his accomplishments; yet he writes with a disarming simplicity, and though humility was not conspicuous among his virtues this by no means proves him to have been wanting in all virtue. A few random headings out of the many hundreds under which he sets forth the grounds of his gratitude to the Almighty are here given.

(1) That he committed the Koran to memory at the age of eight.

(2) That he was miraculously saved from drowning in the Nile as a boy by a crocodile which he mistook for a rock.

(3) That he was never ignorantly bigoted in his attachment to any belief.

(4) That Shaikh al-Islām Zakariyā' (al-Ansārī, d.916/1511 or 926/1521) gave him permission to teach *fiqh* (religious law).

(5) That he composed many books on canon law, mostly original and unprecedented.

(6) That all his teachers of Law and Sufism died content with him.

(7) That from his childhood days he never had any regard for alchemy.

(8) That he had always been averse to eating anything he had been given on the grounds of his being a Sufi or a righteous man.

(9) That he had been compassionate in his dealings with all Muslims, even his bitterest enemies.

(10) That he had been aware of the times in which he was born, and had never attempted to live in the past or the future.

(11) That in all times of hardship he had fled to God and not to men.

(12) That he had lived all his days in circumstances of poverty and self-denial.

(13) That he had never used publicly his powers of foretelling the future.

(14) That he had been preserved by God from the commission of all indecent acts.

(15) That from the age of forty he had not been assailed by any temptation to sin.

(16) That he had never disclosed to any man the inward trials by which he had been afflicted, such as at times caused smoke to issue from his mouth and nostrils.

(17) That from his childhood he had consorted with learned men.

(18) That he had been preserved from the necessity of begging all his life.

(19) That he had never sought worldly rank and preferment.

(20) That he possessed the miraculous faculty of television, of which he gives instances.

(21) That he abstained from marrying his teacher's daughter, out of respect for him and for no other reason.

(22) That his food had often been miraculously multiplied when he was entertaining guests.

(23) That the Jinns had obeyed him from the beginning of his Sufi career.

(24) That he had always been exceedingly wary of the Devil during his mystical progress.

(25) That he had never frequented the houses of rulers, except out of lawful necessity.

(26) That he had always been averse to public praise, whether in prose or verse.

(27) That he had been believed in by many Jinns, Jews and Christians.

(28) That he had miraculously heard beasts and inanimate things praising God.

(29) That he had always been kind to cats and dogs, often giving them a whole chicken if they were hungry.

(30) That he had never forgotten to pray at the appointed times.

(31) That he had been averse to the breaking of wind in the mosque, whether on his own part or another's.

(32) That he had always been present with God, as much when he lay with his wife as when he prayed.

(33) That he had never unduly prolonged his visit to any friend, "a rare virtue in these days."

(34) That he had never changed his feelings towards a disciple when the latter visited a rival.

(35) That he had always felt aversion to having his hand kissed.

(36) That he respected all those who plied a useful and honourable trade.

(37) That his illnesses had never lasted long.

(38) That he had frequently associated with the dead during his sleep and questioned them on their circumstances in the other world.

(39) That he had seen dead saints and been courteously received by them.

(40) That many governors and others had had dreams which had increased their belief in him.

The following are some examples of Al-Sha'rānī's wonderful dreams.

There used to be a person living in our neighbourhood who was scornful of his fellows. God afflicted him with asthma and paralysis, and he continued thus for about ten years, unable to lay his side to the ground; his chin rested on his knee, and his muscles withered away. So he died, and so he was buried. I saw him after his death, and asked him, 'Are you still paralysed?' He replied, 'Yes, and I shall be raised up like this too, and mostly on account of you and Shaikh Shu'aib the Preacher.' When I told this to Shaikh Shu'aib, he remarked, 'Yes, it is quite true. Whenever I passed him, he would blow his nose and throw the phlegm in my face as a mark of contempt.' As for myself, whenever I passed him he would address me in terms not fit to be spoken to a cowherd. God forgive him and be gracious to him!

I used not to give out any charity after the fast, because I had no worldly possessions on the night of the festival and the following day; whatever God gave me being dedicated to the poor who resided with me. In the year 955/1548 I had a vision of myself in a desert place, with a great concourse of the faithful; and I saw something resembling a bolster, the size of a water-melon, lying before each. I saw one of them throw his up to the sky, and then it returned to the ground. I also threw up mine, and it too fell down again. I said to an angel whom I saw there, 'What are these things that are being cast up towards heaven?' He replied, 'The fast of Ramadan; all of these have not given out their charity for breaking the fast, and so their fast is not lifted up to heaven, for this only happens if the faster gives out the charity on breaking the fast.' I said to the angel, 'But I have nothing.' The angel answered, 'Yes you have; there is a clog in a chest, and a second shirt besides the one you are wearing. Sell one of these, and buy something to give out in charity. One like you ought not to labour cheaply.' I asked my children about the clog, and they said, 'We have a clog in the chest; it is for 'Abd al-Rahmān when he grows up.' I sold it to one of my friends, and bought some corn with the proceeds and gave that away.

One of the encounters I had with Sīdī 'Umar ibn al-Fārid was that I went to visit his shrine one day at the

siesta, and called the attendant, but he did not answer me;
and the gate was locked. I therefore recited the *Fātiha*[6]
outside the gate, and returned home. That night he came
to me wearing a great turban and a green woollen robe;
he prayed two *rak'as* with me in the Madrasa of Umm
Khwand, and then said, 'Forgive me, my brother, that I
was not at home; but

Ample repayment is it, one for one.' [7]

I had never heard this half-verse before. Then I knew how
exceedingly devout and noble he was, and that he was one
of the great saints, because he was free to move abroad
and was not confined in his tomb."

One of my encounters with Ibrāhīm al-Dasūqī [8] was
that he came to me and said, 'Visit me, for God's sake.'
So I visited him; and he came to me out of his grave, and
took off his turban and put it upon me, placing my
turban on his knees for an hour. After that he said to me,
'I have come down to you from reciting Traditions and
lecturing on Theology in the Prophet's chamber.' I felt
greatly elated at this.

I frequently prayed God to have mercy on Sīdī 'Alī
al-Khauwās at a seance. That night I saw him, and he
was eager to kiss my foot, while I was eager to prevent
him. Then he prevailed over me in an unguarded moment,
and kissed the sole of my foot; and I awoke, with the
softness of his lips still upon the sole of my foot.

The close of the Dark Ages of Islam by no means spelt
the end of Sufi inventiveness. New Religious Orders have
continued to emerge down to modern times; some have
exercised an important influence in international politics.
We will content ourselves by mentioning two of the most
celebrated—the Tijānīya and the Sanūsīya. Of these the
former was founded by Ahmad al-Tijānī (1150-1230/1737-
1815), a native of 'Ain Mādī near Tahmut. As a leading
feature of the teaching of this Order is submission to the
established government, the Tijānīya have in general
enjoyed excellent relations with the French authorities

ever since Algeria was conquered; they have on the whole resisted encouragements and threats from elements aiming at the expulsion of the foreign occupiers.[9] The Sanūsīya, who have had a more turbulent history, owe their origin as a military brotherhood to Sīdī Muhammad al-Sanūsī (1206-76/1791-1859); the part they have played in two world wars suffices to indicate the vast powers which can be concentrated in the hands of religious leaders ambitious to exercise temporal authority; the present Head of the Order claims the rulership of Cyrenaica, and pretensions have been advanced in his name to the whole of Libya.[10]

One of the last Sufi authors of the classical tradition, Shaikh Muhammad Amīn al-Kurdī al-Shāfi'ī al-Naqsha-bandī, a native of Irbil in Iraq, died as recently as 1332/1914; his *Tanwīr al-qulūb* was edited with a biographical note by his "successor" (*khalīfa*) Shaikh Salāma al-'Azzāmī of the Azhar (6th edition, Cairo 1348/1929). The biographer offers a remarkable catalogue of the wonders related of his master. We are told how for some considerable period of his life, whenever he ate with his disciples, although only a little bread was placed before him this was miraculously adequate for the needs of a large company and still some remained over. A rival who was appointed Imam of a certain mosque in preference to him was struck down with paralysis the very night of his appointment, and never recovered. He worked various cures in cases where the doctors had despaired. He was seen in the spirit by his disciples when he was absent in the body—on one occasion so far afield as Mecca, although the shaikh was all the time at Cairo. He many times predicted future events accurately; as when he foretold, many years before it happened, that a certain small state hostile to Islam would suffer a crushing reverse; and that certain students of the Azhar would fail or pass in their examinations. All his last days he was never seen without a fresh mantle of glittering light that dazzled all beholders.

The greater part of the *Tanwīr al-qulūb* is taken up with an account of the principles of Islamic theology and jurisprudence; it is only the third section (pages 404-565) that deals with mysticism, on a somewhat elementary and unoriginal level. Muhammad Amīn traces his *silsila* as a Naqshabandī back to the eponymous founder of the Order, Shāh Naqshaband Bahā' al-Dīn Muhammad b. Muhammad al-Uwaisī al-Bukhārī,[11] and names among his spiritual ancestors the celebrated Indian Scholar Ahmad al-Fārūqī al-Sirhindī, called Mujaddid al-Alf al-Thānī,[12] and his son Muhammad Ma'sūm.[13] The genealogy is taken back from Shāh Naqshaband step by step, through the famous Companion Salmān al-Fārisī and Abū Bakr al-Siddīq the first Caliph, to the prophet Muhammad, Gabriel, and God.

One of the most curious sections of the book is that in which the author gives instructions on how to perform the *dhikr qalbī* (commemoratio cordis). The *dhikr* is divided into two parts; the first is in the Name of the Essence (*Allāh*), the second is by way of negation (*lā ilāha*) and asseveration (*illa 'llāh*); the whole formula making up the first article of the Muslim confession of faith ("There is no god but God"). It comprises eleven preparatory exercises (*ādāb*), as follows.

(1) Perform the ritual purification.

(2) Pray two *rak'as*.

(3) Face the *qibla* (Mecca) in a deserted place.

(4) Squat upon the folded legs, as at prayer.

(5) Ask forgiveness of all sins, while picturing all your misdeeds as assembled simultaneously before you in God's sight.

(6) Recite the *Fātiha*[14] once, and the *Ikhlās*[15] thrice,

offering them to the spirit of Muhammad and the spirits of all the Naqshabandī shaikhs.

(7) Close the eyes; keep the lips tightly sealed; and press the tongue against the roof of your mouth; to make your humility perfect and to exclude all visual disturbances.

(8) Perform the "grave exercise," i.e. imagine that you are dead, that you have been washed, wrapped in your winding-sheet and laid in your tomb, and that all the mourners have departed, leaving you alone to face the Judgment.

(9) Perform the "guide exercise," when the neophyte's heart confronts the heart of his shaikh, keeping his image in mind even though he be absent, seeking the shaikh's blessing, and as it were passing away (*fanā'*) in him.

(10) Concentrate all your bodily senses, expel all preoccupations and wayward impulses of the heart, and direct all your perception towards God. Then say, "O God, Thou art my Quest, and Thy Pleasure is my desire." Then commemorate the Name of the Essence within the heart, recalling that God is present, watching and encompassing you.

(11) Await the "visitation" (*wārid*, i.e. spiritual epiphenomenon) of the *dhikr* when it is over for a little while before opening your eyes.

The author furnishes a brief description of the psychic organs.

The *qalb* (heart) is two fingers' breadth below the left nipple towards the side; it is shaped like a pine-cone. It is under the foot (sc. religious control) of Adam; its light is yellow.

The *rūh* (spirit) is two fingers' breadth below the right nipple towards the breast. It is under the foot of Noah and Abraham; its light is red.

The *sirr* (inmost conscience) is two fingers' breadth

above the left nipple towards the breast. It is under the foot of Moses; its light is white.

The *khafī* (hidden depth) is two fingers' breadth above the right nipple towards the breast. It is beneath the foot of Jesus; its light is black.

The *akhfā* (most hidden depth) is in the middle of the breast. It is under the foot of Muhammad; its light green.

This being all explained, Muhammad Amīn proceeds to instruct on how to meditate the *dhikr* formula *lā ilāha illa 'llāh*.

Keep the tongue fixed firmly to the roof of the mouth. After drawing a deep breath, you should hold it, and make a beginning with the word *lā*. Imagine that you are taking it from below the navel; let it extend along the organs enumerated above, and finally bring it up to the "rational soul" (*al-nafs al-nātiqa*) which is in the first lobe of the brain. Follow this up by taking the *hamza* of *ilāha*—in imagination—from the brain, then let it descend until it finishes at the right shoulder-blade; then draw it down to the *rūh*. Now imagine that you are taking the *hamza* of *illa 'llāh* from the shoulder-blade; let it slide down the edge of the middle of the breast until it finishes at the *qalb*, which may be imagined at this point as beating to the Word of Majesty, with all the force of the pent-up breath pressing against the core of the heart, until its effect and heat are felt throughout the body. Its heat will burn up all the corrupt particles in the body, while the sound particles will be irradiated by the Light of Majesty. This process is to be repeated twenty-one times, not automatically but reflectively and with due regard to the meaning of the formula meditated. At the end of his exertions, the commemorator (*dhākir*) will experience the result of his *dhikr qalbī*; he will lose all consciousness of being a man and a part of creation, and will be entirely destroyed in the attraction of the Divine Essence.

Sufism, in its original as in its derived forms, may now be said to have come to an end as a movement dominating the minds and hearts of learned and earnest men. Yet its mark lies ineradicably athwart the pages of Muslim literature; the technical vocabulary of the Sufis, with all the psychological subtlety of its terms, can scarcely be eliminated from the language of modern philosophy and science. When so original and revolutionary a thinker as the late Sir Muhammad Iqbal desired to popularise his ideas of Man and Superman, not only did he turn back to Rūmī and the mediaeval mystics to discover antecedents within Islam for the system for which he sought acceptance, but he cast his thoughts in the mould of Sufi allegory that has been sanctified by centuries of Persian poetry.

> In my heart's empire, see
> How he rides spitefully,
> Rides with imperious will
> To ravage, and to kill!
>
> No heart is there, but bright
> Gleameth in that moon's light,
> A thousand mirrors, see!
> Reflect his coquetry.
>
> To each hand he hath won
> Ten realms of Solomon,
> Yet gambles with it all
> To gain a mean, poor thrall.
>
> The hearts of such as know
> Swift he assaults; but lo!
> Before the unwise, unskilled
> He casteth down his shield.[16]

TWELVE

EPILOGUE

THE wheel now appears to have turned full circle. Sufism has run its course; and in the progress of human thought it is illusory to imagine that there can ever be a return to the point of departure. A new journey lies ahead for humanity to travel. Some men at all events will be seeking to walk along that road in the company of God. Some Muslims will desire to recapture in their own hearts the ecstatic joy experienced by those Sufis of old, to comfort and confirm them:

> Within an age become exceeding strange,
> Cruel, and terrible, wherein we need
> Most urgently a statement of our faith
> And intellectual arguments thereto.

If the "intellectual arguments" must of necessity be of a different order from those which satisfied al-Junaid, al-Ghazālī, Ibn 'Arabī, Jalāl al-Dīn Rūmī, it by no means follows that the discipline of body and spirit invented by the Sufi masters will prove inadequate to meet the requirements of the modern and future man.

It is far from useless to look back into the pages of the distant past. Whether we are Muslims or not, we are all surely children of One Father; and it is therefore no impertinence, no irrelevancy for the Christian scholar to aim at rediscovering those vital truths which made the Sufi movement so powerful an influence for good. If he may have the co-operation of his Muslim colleagues in this research—and signs are not wanting that he will—together they may hope to unfold a truly remarkable and inspiring history of high human endeavour; together they

may succeed in retracing a pattern of thought and behaviour which will supply the needs of many seeking the
re-establishment of moral and spiritual values in these
dark and threatening times.

NOTES

CHAPTER 1. For a general bibliography of Sufi studies, see my *Introduction to the History of Sufism* (Longmans, 1943).

CHAPTER 2. (1) Kor. 96:1. (2) Kor. 74:1. (3) Kor. 1:3. (4) Kor. 2:256. (5) Kor. 88:17. (6) Kor. 16:81. (7) Kor. 16:71. (8) Kor. 2:159. (9) Kor. 2:24. (10) Kor. 2:182. (11) Kor. 50:15. (12) Kor. 29:19. (13) Kor. 2:109. (14) Kor. 24:35-42. (15) Kor. 21:49. (16) Kor. 21:52. (17) Kor. 21:79, 81. (18) Kor. 20:8-14. (19) Kor. 7:139. (20) Kor. 17:1. (21) Kor. 53:4-18. (22) Kor. 2:27-32. (23) Kor. 7:171. (24) Kor. 96:19. (25) Kor. 9:119. (26) Kor. 5:119. (27) Kor. 5:59. (28) Kor. 8:17. (29) Kor. 55:26.

CHAPTER 3. (1) Hitti, *History of the Arabs* p.395. (2) Hujwīrī, *Kashf al-mahjūb* (tr. Nicholson) p.19. (3) Kor. 57:19. (4) Kor. 20:131. (5) Kharrāz, *Kitāb al-Sidq* (tr. Arberry) p.18. (6) Ibid. p.23. (7) Ahmad b. Hanbal, *Musnad* I p.30,52. (8) Kor. 5:119. (9) Qushairī, *Risāla* p.88. (10) Kor. 5:59. (11) Kharrāz, op.cit. p.6, 40; Nicholson, *Mystics of Islam* p.100; Massignon, *Essai* p.106. (12) Nicholson, op.cit. p.68. (13) Ibid. p.80. (14) Ibid. p.83. (15) Massignon, op.cit. p.107. (16) Nicholson, op.cit. p.53. (17) Ibid. p.51. (18) Hujwīrī, op.cit. p.267. (19) Ibid. p.277. (20) Kalābādhī, *al-Ta'arruf* (tr. Arberry) pp.26-7. (21) Hujwīrī, op.cit. p.283. (22) Ibid. p.302.

CHAPTER 4. (1) Kharrāz, op.cit. pp.20-1. (2) Abū Nu'aim, *Hilya* II pp. 134-40. (3) Massignon, op.cit. pp.175-6. (4) Ibid. p.131. (5) Ibid. pp.132-4. (6) Abū Nu'aim, op.cit. VII p.368. (7) Ibid. VIII p.29. (8) Ibid. VIII p.17. (9) Ibid. VIII p.16. (10) Ibid. VIII p.35. (11) Ibid. VIII pp.18-19. (12) Massignon, op.cit. p.228. (13) Abū Nu'aim, op.cit. VIII p.59. (14) Ibid. VIII pp.60-1. (15) Brockelmann, *Geschichte der arabischen Litteratur* (Supplement) I p.256. (16) Abū Nu'aim. op.cit. VIII p.336. (17) Ibid. VIII p.346. (18) Ibid. VIII p.348. (19) Ibid. VIII pp.342-3. (20) Ibid. VIII p.346. (21) Ibid. VIII p.85. (22) Ibid. VIII p.100. (23) 'Attār, *Tadhkirat al-auliyā'* I p.66 (quoted by M. Smith, *Early Mysticism* p.186). (24) Kalābādhī, op.cit. p.159. (25) Nicholson, op.cit. p.115. (26) Nicholson in *Legacy of Islam* pp.213-4. (27) Brockelmann, op.cit. (Suppl.) I p.351; Massignon, op.cit. p.204. (28) Abū Nu'aim, op.cit. IX p.254.

CHAPTER 5. (1) Kalābādhī, op.cit. pp.2-3. (2) Brockelmann, op.cit. (Suppl.) I p.352. (3) Abū Nu'aim, op.cit. X p.74. (4) Edited by M. Smith (Gibb Memorial New Series), 1940. (5) Edited by A. J. Arberry (Cairo, 1937). (6) Abū Nu'aim, op.cit. X pp.78-9. (7) Ibid. IX p.342. (8) Ibid. IX p.390. (9) Partly preserved in Sarrāj, *al-Luma'* pp.380-9. (10) Hujwīrī, op.cit. p.238. (11) Sarrāj, op.cit. p.382. (12) See e.g. Hujwīrī, op.cit. p.242. (13) See edition and translation by A. J. Arberry. (14) Kharrāz, op.cit. p.66. (15) Contained in MS. Sehit Ali 1374 (Istanbul), see Massignon, op.cit. pp.273-4; A. J. Arberry in *J.R.A.S.* (1935) p.499. An edition and translation has been prepared by my former pupil Dr. Ali Abdel Kader. (16) Qushairī, op.cit. p.3, 136;

Hujwīrī, op.cit. p.281. (17) Kor. 7:166-7. (18) I quote Dr. Abdel Kader's translation. (19) See above, p.27. (20) Qushairī, op.cit. p.126. (21) Kor. 55:26. (22) Sarrāj, op.cit. p.212. (23) Quoted in Nicholson, *Idea of Personality* p.32. (24) Nicholson in *Legacy of Islam* p.217. (25) See below, p.101. (26) Abū Nu'aim, op.cit. X p.61. (27) Ibid. X p.61. (28) Kalābādhī, op.cit. p.87. (29) Ibid. p.96. (30) Ibid. p.100.

CHAPTER 6. (1) Edited and translated by A. J. Arberry (Gibb Memorial New Series), 1935. (2) See above, p.55. (3) Niffarī, *Mawāqif* p.52. (4) Hujwīrī, op.cit. p.176. (5) Ibid. p.xiv. (6) Edited by R. A. Nicholson (Gibb Memorial Series), 1914; Supplementary pages edited by A. J. Arberry, 1947. (7) Abū Tālib al-Makkī, *Qūt al-qulūb* I p.160. (8) Edited by A. J. Arberry (Cairo, 1934); transl. as *The Doctrine of the Sūfīs* (C.U.P. 1935). (9) Edition by J. Pedersen in progress. (10) Edited by A. E. Affifi (Alexandria, 1944). (11) Translated by R. A. Nicholson (Gibb Memorial Series), 1911. (12) Translated by A. J. Arberry in *Islamic Culture* (1936) pp.369-89.

CHAPTER 7. (1) Qushairī, op.cit. p.7. (2) Cf. Hujwīrī, op.cit. p.294. (3) Kor. 29:69. (4) Cf. Hujwīrī, op.cit. p.200. (5) Kor. 2:150. (6) Kor. 65:3. (7) Kor. 14:7. (8) Kor. 5:119. (9) See above, p.21, and cf. Hujwīrī, op.cit. p.182. (10) Kor. 68:4. (11) Kor. 10:63. (12) Kor. 40:62. (13) Cf. p.21 above. (14) Nicholson, *Mystics of Islam* pp.28-9. (15) Quoted in Nicholson, *Idea of Personality* pp.39-40. (16) Wensinck, *La Pensée de Ghazzali*, p.111.

CHAPTER 8. (1) Nicholson, *Studies in Islamic Mysticism* pp.21-2. (2) Lane, *Manners and Customs of the Modern Egyptians* (1st ed.) II pp.172-4. (3) Ibid. II pp.201-3. (4) The "Chief Shaikh" of the Sufis of Egypt, a hereditary title. (5) Prayer-carpet. (6) Demented. (7) Thus, the Shādhilī Order specialised in drinking coffee, an Arabic word (*qahwa*) originally signifying a sort of wine.

CHAPTER 9. (1) Nicholson, *Idea of Personality* pp.44-5. (2) Nicholson, *Studies* p.167. (3) Ibid. pp.170-1. (4) Ibid. pp.228-9. (5) Jāmī, *Nofahāt al-uns* p.634. (6) Sha'rānī, *al-Tabaqāt al-kubrā*. (7) Brockelmann, op.cit. (Suppl.) I pp.791-802. (8) Ibn 'Arabī, *Tarjumān al-ashwāq* (ed. Nicholson) pp.49-50. (9) Summarised from A. E. Affifi, *The Mystical Philosophy of Muhyid Din-Ibnul 'Arabī*. (10) Ibn 'Arabī, *Fusūs al-hikam* p.106. (11) Ibn 'Arabī, *al-Futūhā* a.-Makkīya II p.65. (12) Ibid. I p.319. (13) Nicholson, *Studies* p.84.

CHAPTER 10. (1) See Vol. VIII of Nicholson's edition, p.418 (index). (2) A. J. Arberry, *Immortal Rose* p.70. (3) Edited by R. A. Nicholson, 1905-7. (4) Translated by R. T. H. Griffith (1882) and A. Rogers (1892). (5) Translated into French by Chézy (1805), into German by Hartmann (1807). (6) R. A. Nicholson, *A Persian Forerunner of Dante*. (7) A. J. Arberry, *Fifty Poems of Hāfiz* pp. 31-2. (8) For details see A. J. Arberry, *British Contributions to Persian Studies*, especially pp.18-30.

CHAPTER 11. (1) Edited and translated by Mahfūz al-Haqq (Calcutta 1929). (2) Taufīq al-Tawīl, *al-Tasauwuf fī Misr* p.47. (3) Ibid. p.50. (4) Ibid. p.143. (5) J. Schacht in *Encyclopaedia of Islam* IV p.319. (6) Sura 1 of the Koran. (7) Part of a ritual prayer. (8) The Egyptian Sufi who died in 919/1514. (9) See *Encylopaedia of Islam* IV pp.745-6. (10) See ibid. IV pp.154-5. (11) Died in 791/1389. (12) Author of a collection of Sufi letters, died in 1034/1624. (13) Son of Ahmad al-Fārūqī, also author of Sufi letters. (14) See Note 6 above. (15) Sura 112 of the Koran. (16) Iqbāl, *Zabūr-i 'Ajam* I p.31.

INDEX